PAST&REPAST

The History and Hospitality of the Missouri Governor's Mansion

Governor Bond

*Governor and Mrs.
Christopher Samuel Bond
and their son, Samuel
Reid Bond.*

FOREWORD

The "People's Mansion" is the term Kit and I often use in describing the Governor's Mansion because it belongs to all the people of the state, and we are only temporary residents. Without question, our greatest pleasure while living in the house has been sharing it with others.

When Kit first ran for Governor in 1972, I promised we would open the Mansion to the public, and we did in April of 1973. Since then, on Tuesdays and Thursdays, thousands of people have enjoyed the beauty, traditions, history and hospitality of a truly remarkable house. Perched on the bluffs overlooking the Missouri River, the Mansion with its distinctive mansard roof and grillwork is a familiar landmark in Jefferson City and a tangible element of our Missouri heritage.

Recognizing the need to preserve the historic 1871 Governor's Mansion for future generations, I established Missouri Mansion Preservation, Inc. in 1974. This statewide nonpartisan organization, in addition to providing an important oversight function, assists the state in the restoration of the building and in acquisition of period furnishings in the Renaissance Revival style. Countless Missourians have responded with their time, talents and financial support, and completion of the first-floor restoration is scheduled to coincide with the traditional Candlelight Tours during the 1983 Christmas season.

PAST & REPAST: The History and Hospitality of the Missouri Governor's Mansion is published not only to document the restoration progress to date and to raise additional funds to complete the restoration, but also to record the rich and colorful history of a magnificent house, designed by one of Missouri's greatest nineteenth-century architects, George Ingham Barnett.

Through the lives of the twenty-eight Governors and First Families who have resided and entertained in the Mansion, there emerges a Missouri tradition of hospitality. We attempt in this book to give you a flavor of the past, and we offer a potpourri of tastes to enjoy today.

PAST & REPAST is the history of a wonderful house; it also reflects our approach to food preparation and entertaining. Fresh seasonal ingredients, simply prepared and artistically presented, are just as welcome at the family dinner table as at a Victorian repast or a state dinner at the Governor's Mansion.

Carolyn Bond

Missouri Mansion Preservation, Inc. gratefully acknowledges the generous support of the Whitaker Foundation, Urban C. Bergbauer, Trustee, for the publication of PAST & REPAST.

PAST & REPAST

The History and Hospitality of the Missouri Governor's Mansion

Missouri Mansion Preservation, Inc. ❧ Jefferson City, Missouri

Additional copies of *PAST & REPAST* may be obtained by writing:

PAST & REPAST
Missouri Mansion Preservation, Inc.
Post Office Box 1133
Jefferson City, Missouri 65102

Enclose your return address with a check payable to MMPI/*PAST & REPAST* in the amount of $15 per copy plus $2 postage and handling for each book.

First Edition
First Printing: 10,000 copies   October, 1983
Second Printing: 10,000 copies November, 1983
Third Printing: 10,000 copies   January, 1984

Printed in the United States of America by The Lowell Press, Inc. of Kansas City, Missouri.

Missouri Mansion Preservation, Inc. is a statewide, nonpartisan, not-for-profit corporation that assists the State of Missouri with the restoration and historical interpretation of the 1871 Executive Mansion in Jefferson City. Founded in 1974, MMPI has raised more than $1,000,000 in donations of cash and furnishings for the Mansion. Proceeds from the sale of *PAST & REPAST* will be used for the Mansion's continuing restoration and educational programs.

TABLE OF CONTENTS

HISTORY

A cold wind whipped across the river and swept against the treeless bluff where the tall red brick Mansion stood. The windows on the north side rattled, but inside the sound was muffled by the lilting strains of a popular waltz performed by Professor Mahler's orchestra. The house already was filled with guests and more were arriving every minute, alighting from carriages and clutching tightly to their hats and cloaks as they hurried toward the huge front doors.

It was Wednesday evening, January 24, 1872, and Governor B. Gratz Brown of Missouri and his wife, Mary, were holding a grand ball to celebrate the official opening of the new Executive Mansion.

Dignitaries from all over the state had gathered for the event. One hundred and fifty guests from St. Louis alone had braved the bad weather to join the festivities. Gentlemen wore their finest suits, and "the ladies shone like a Louis XV salon," according to a Jefferson City newspaper. Their gowns, ordered weeks in advance, were fashioned of silks, satins and laces, and their hair was teased and coaxed into elaborate styles. Hairdressers were in great demand, and some of the ladies reportedly had slept sitting up several nights before the ball to keep from damaging their coiffures.

At the entrance servants took the guests' wraps. The sliding doors separating the rooms on the first floor had been pushed back to create a spacious hall. The crowd, "estimated at from 1,500 to 2,000," was so great that it was difficult to pass from the Great Hall into the Double Parlor or from the Double Parlor into the Dining Room.

Oldest photograph of present Executive Mansion, just before occupancy, December 1871.

Members of the State Guard, clad in uniforms with brass buttons and shiny epaulets, circulated among the guests who were dancing in the Great Hall and on the second-floor landing.

In the ballroom on the third floor, long tables loaded with delicacies, including "a pyramid of spitted snipe," had been set up by the St. Louis caterers. Punch was served, but no alcohol, and it was rumored that some of the newspaper reporters present had fortified themselves for the festivities during frequent visits to the nearby Madison Hotel.

The principal topic of conversation that evening was the Mansion: In all of Jefferson City and for miles around there was not another structure like it. Designed by an Englishman with an eye for classical proportion, it dwarfed all the other residences in the capital city. The rooms on the first and second floors had 17-foot ceilings. The Grand Stairway curved elegantly upward from the Great Hall. The double walnut doors at the front entrance each weighed several hundred pounds, but were so delicately balanced on their German silver hinges that they could be opened by a child.

This splendid Mansion, dramatically located on the bluffs overlooking one of America's great rivers, was evidence that Missouri had progressed from the frontier era through the struggles of development and the trials of conflict to prosperous maturity.

Here is the story of that Mansion and the events and personalities that left their imprint upon its history and hospitality.

Many cultures and nationalities have contributed to the unique heritage of Missouri. Long before the white man arrived, American Indian tribes like the Osage, the Missouri and the Sac and Fox built sizable towns along the river bottomlands and carried on trade and intermittent warfare with one another.

Two-thirds of the land was covered with rolling, tall-grass prairie that supported a seemingly inexhaustible population of antelope and buffalo. The big rivers teemed with fish; along the tributary creeks and streams lived beaver, mink and otter. In the hardwood forests to the south, along the steep hills later to be known as the Ozarks, could be found deer, wild turkeys and black bears. It was a land rich with abundant game, fertile soil and plentiful mineral deposits.

Representatives of France were the first white men to recognize the land's potential. In the late seventeenth century, from Canada and the Great Lakes, the legendary *voyageurs* Marquette, Joliet and La Salle paddled down the Mississippi River in search of its mouth. These explorers opened the heartland of the continent to the frontiersman. By the early decades of the eighteenth century, other Frenchmen journeyed to the new land and founded permanent communities. Fort Orleans on the Missouri River was established by Sieur de Bourgmond in the 1720s in response to a threat of invasion by Spaniards from New Mexico. Sometime before the middle of the century, French settlers founded the community of Ste. Genevieve. Upriver, in 1764, Pierre Laclede and Auguste Chouteau helped found St. Louis, which soon became a thriving fur-trade center.

During its first 50 years of settlement by Europeans, Missouri was thoroughly French. Men and women of Gallic ancestry traveled down from Canada or upriver from New Orleans and built villages on the bluffs and flatlands overlooking the Mississippi. Their houses were of *poteaux-en-terre* construction—upright posts set in the ground with clay and rubble packed in the wall spaces, and the entire house, in some instances, girdled by a *galerie* or porch. The customs they brought with them, the love of music and fancy dress and tasty food, are a colorful part of Missouri's history.

The close of the French and Indian War brought important changes in the Mississippi Valley. The lands west of the river were ceded by France to Spain and the British claimed the largely unsettled territory east to the Appalachian Mountains. To avoid living under British rule, many French families from the communities of Cahokia and Kaskaskia moved west across the river. Later, the Revolutionary War touched Missouri only marginally. A British attack on St. Louis was repulsed by a force of French and Spanish militia supported by American colonists and their Indian allies.

The following years were relatively peaceful, but distrustful of foreign intruders, the rulers of the new Spanish interior closed off the Mississippi and its vital outlet at New Orleans to American trade. Fur pelts and agricultural goods at ports on the upper river were left to rot on wharves and in warehouses. To continue in trade, many Americans applied for and received sizable land grants on the Spanish side of the river. George Morgan of Philadelphia established a colony at New Madrid in 1789, and other settlers from the East founded similar communities. By 1800 more than half the 10,000 people living west of the river were Americans of English descent. They brought their own style of life to the new land—a taste for wild game, gambling and hard whiskey—and their customs mingled with those of the French and Spanish, contributing to the cosmopolitan flavor of the area.

Meanwhile, the new emperor of France, Napoleon Bonaparte, was hoping to recover France's colonial empire in the Mississippi Valley. The Treaty of San Ildefonso (1800) returned the territory to France, but not for long. Military reverses in Europe and the New World—in particular, the successful campaign waged by Toussaint L'Overture against the French army in Haiti—caused Napoleon to change his mind. In 1803 American representatives in Paris were notified that the emperor was prepared to sell France's New World possessions. The issue of a free port at the mouth of the Mississippi was critical to American interests: Whoever controlled New Orleans controlled the fate of American commerce throughout the heartland. A price of 60 million francs ($15,000,000) was agreed on and in December 1803 the United States took formal possession of the territory through the Louisiana Purchase. On March 9, 1804, with an American contingent (including Meriwether Lewis of the famed Lewis and Clark Expedition of 1804-1806) looking on, the French tricolor was lowered for the last time in St. Louis, and the Stars and Stripes was raised in its place.

Initially, all of the new American territory was known simply as Louisiana, as it had been named by La Salle to honor Louis

William Clark,
Territorial Governor and
leader of the Lewis and
Clark Expedition, portrait
by Chester Harding.

XIV. In 1804 Congress divided the territory into two parts, with a Governor in New Orleans and another in St. Louis. President Thomas Jefferson appointed both executives, and for the St. Louis post selected as temporary Governor Amos Stoddard, who served from March 10 to September 30, 1804. From July 1805 to August 1806, James Wilkinson held the post. Wilkinson incurred the suspicion and hostility of many territorial residents because of his preferential treatment of French landowners and his love of military rule. He was replaced by Meriwether Lewis who never formally took office. A moody and enigmatic man, he died under mysterious circumstances in a Tennessee roadhouse in 1809, a victim of murder or by his own hand.

In 1812 lower Louisiana became a state, and the upper territory for the first time was officially named Missouri.

By 1815 the population had reached 20,000; six years later when statehood was achieved, it had jumped to 70,000. While Missouri's population was increasing, the westward flow of land-hungry pioneers was beginning. Until the end of the century Missouri was to be the conduit through which many of them passed to the Great Plains and beyond.

Benjamin Howard, who succeeded Meriwether Lewis, resigned as Governor in 1813 and was replaced by the popular William Clark, the other leader of the Lewis and Clark Expedition. Clark lived with his young wife and family in several successive residences in St. Louis before finally settling in a two-story brick house on Main Street. For several years this house served as the Governor's official residence. A large room at the east end became known as the Council Chamber, and it was there that Clark entertained important tribal chiefs. It was an imposing room, more than 100 feet long, crammed with curios and artifacts, including birchbark canoes, piles of mastadon bones and a 12-foot-long crocodile skin.

Missouri became a state on August 10, 1821, a day of jubilation and rejoicing for its citizens. St. Charles was designated as the temporary seat of government, and the first elected Governor, Alexander McNair, traveled there on horseback from his home in St. Louis to meet with the legislature, living in rented rooms in a rock house near the buildings that served as the first state capitol.

The first First Lady, the former Marguerite de Reilhe, was born in St. Louis and educated by her father, a French nobleman. In 1824 she helped form the first St. Louis female charitable society, an interdenominational group which met at her home.

Frederick Bates, McNair's successor, lived in a beautiful house on a thousand-acre estate, Thornhill, overlooking the Missouri River 20 miles from St. Louis. When state affairs called him to St. Charles, Bates stepped into a boat at the foot of his property, crossed the river and entered a waiting carriage for the short, three-mile drive to the capital. A virtual recluse, he refused to travel to St. Louis to greet the Marquis de Lafayette when the Revolutionary War hero made a state visit in April of 1825 (the sum of $37 allocated from city funds covered all the entertainment costs). Bates died of pleurisy three months later after serving a year in office. He was replaced by the President Pro Tempore of the Senate, Abraham J.

First state capitol, 1821,
St. Charles.

Williams, a bachelor shoemaker from Columbia who served until January 1826 but never moved to the capital.

A provision in the first state constitution decreed that the permanent capital should be located in the center of the state along the Missouri River within 40 miles of the mouth of the Osage River. A settlement date of 1826 was established, and a committee was soon on its way upriver to choose the site. Twenty-five hundred acres of land in an area of broken bluffs and bottomlands 12 miles west of the mouth of the Osage was finally selected. At first the choice did not appear advantageous. One contemporary account said the area was "too poor to support any considerable population or extensive resettlement." At the time of its selection, the soon-to-be City of Jefferson had one resident—a dramshop owner who plied thirsty river travelers with rum and whiskey.

On a bluff 200 feet above the Missouri River, a substantial brick structure was completed in November of 1826. The exterior measured 60 by 40 feet, and the two stories contained 10 rooms. A glowing description of the new Governor's residence/capitol which appeared in a Jefferson City newspaper called it "A spacious and well-constructed building . . . the workmanship . . . is not to be surpassed in the state." Although later accounts reported the building to have been more modest, it cost nearly $20,000 and "was the first tangible symbol of permanent state government in Missouri."

Jefferson City in the late 1820s was a raw frontier town, "a struggling village, where Indians camped in close proximity, and wolves howled around the doors at night." Game was plentiful;

First executive residence/capitol building, 1826, Jefferson City.

Second executive residence, 1834, Jefferson City.

meals offered in a local hostelry included venison, bear meat, turkeys, wild honey, potatoes, Indian bread and fricasseed plover. Twice a year, on horseback or on foot or by riverboat, lawmakers made their way to the capital. The Senate met on the second story of the new brick building, the House of Representatives on the ground floor. The bachelor Governor, John Miller, lived in two rooms in the northwest corner. They were a lively group. The downstairs hall where the representatives met was frequently used as a ballroom, and on weekends the walls resounded with the music of Virginia reels, waltzes and polkas. Although satisfied with his own arrangements, Governor Miller was concerned about the limited accommodations for families and pressed for new executive quarters.

Miller's successor, Daniel Dunklin, was determined not to bring his family to Jefferson City until new quarters were built. Three months after his election in August 1832, the Missouri legislature appropriated $5,000 for a new Governor's residence. Construction began in the fall of 1833, and although delayed by a cholera epidemic, was completed early the following year. The house was at the south end of the same block as the capitol. It was a rectangular structure with wings, 48 by 30 feet, built of limestone blocks with a two-story portico supported by four stone columns. The three rooms on the first floor were connected by folding doors so they could be opened to form a larger area for entertaining; the kitchen was a separate out-building. During the Dunklins' term in office "the full cycle of family events—the birth, death and marriage of children" took place in the first official executive residence.

Early Jefferson City with its new capitol, 1840.

Lilburn Boggs was Governor from 1836 to 1840. Boggs and his wife, Panthea, a granddaughter of Daniel Boone, were the first to hold an Inaugural Reception and also introduced the custom of inviting legislators to dinner alphabetically in small groups. Even with the three rooms open on the ground floor, the area was still too small for large gatherings.

Governor Boggs appealed twice to the legislature to sell the new residence and build a more commodious home for the First Family. His second appeal followed the fire of November 15, 1837, when the first capitol was destroyed. Wet blankets applied hastily to the roof of the adjacent executive residence saved it from destruction, and no one was injured. The real loss was the destruction of state and county records dating back several decades.

During the administration of Thomas Reynolds (1840-1844), fire again threatened to destroy the residence but through the prompt action of a bucket brigade, the fire was doused before much damage occurred. Governor Reynolds' tenure, which began promisingly, ended in disaster. Beset by domestic troubles, he pressed a rifle muzzle to his forehead, and with a piece of twine attached to his finger, pulled the trigger. (A Reynolds sofa with unusual pineapple-shaped legs is one of the oldest pieces of furniture remaining in the Mansion today.)

Lieutenant Governor Meredith Marmaduke completed the remaining nine months of Reynolds' term. Entertaining was curtailed following Reynolds' suicide and the new First Lady, the former Lavinia Sappington, had few social responsibilities. Although the Marmadukes' tenure as First Family was brief, the Saline County Sappington-Marmaduke dynasty had a substantial impact on Missouri history. Lavinia was the daughter of Dr. John Sappington of Arrow Rock who introduced quinine as a remedy for malaria. Her mother was the sister of Kentucky Governor John Breathitt, three of her sisters married Claiborne Fox Jackson who became Governor of Missouri in 1861, her son was elected the twenty-fifth Governor of the state and two of her granddaughters served as official hostesses of the Executive Mansion.

New Governors often found their residence lacking common amenities such as furniture and crockery. John Cummins Edwards, who occupied the house from 1844 to 1848, declared that "to expect the Governor to furnish the House out of his own private funds is out of the question." Because of the paltry appropriations from the legislature, Edwards did so, however, and his donation is still in the Mansion—the Dining Room sideboard decorated with a large star on the front panel and flanked by two circular enclosed cupboards at either end. After completing his term of office, Edwards, a bachelor and still under 40, went to California during the Gold Rush, married and made his fortune as a provision merchant.

Austin A. King, whose wife, Nancy, came from a prestigious Virginia family, followed Edwards into office in 1848, serving until 1853. Before moving to Jefferson City, Mrs. King had established on their Ray County property a school to educate the children of slaves, although it was against the law of the period. Historical records noted that the Kings "gave splendid entertainments

Lithograph of Jefferson Landing, c. 1850, and steamboat era on the Missouri River.

with refreshments," which implied wine or spirits. Twice during their tenure, Jefferson City was ravaged by cholera, one of the most dreaded nineteenth-century diseases.

At the end of the King administration, the inaugural ceremonies were moved from November or December of the election year to January of the following year.

A hero of the Mexican War, General Sterling Price returned to Missouri in 1848, and was elected Governor four years later. Price moved his family to Jefferson City from their family farm, Val Verde, in Chariton County. The charitable nature of the First Family was evident during the 1855 train disaster. Following the collapse of the Gasconade River Bridge under the weight of the first Pacific Railroad train en route to Jefferson City, Governor and Mrs. Price led in comforting the injured and the bereaved. After leaving office, Price joined the Confederate Army during the Civil War and later established a colony for Confederate exiles in Carlota, Mexico.

Four Governors, the most in any one year in the state's history, presided over Missouri's fortunes during 1857. The changes came so swiftly that Jefferson Citians barely had time to pay a courtesy call on one First Lady before she was replaced by another.

Trusten Polk was inaugurated January 5, succeeding Sterling Price. Eight days after he was sworn in, the legislature elected Polk to the United States Senate. He resigned as Governor on

February 27 after serving 53 days, the shortest term in Missouri history. Polk resigned from the Senate in 1861 to serve with Price during the Civil War and later joined his followers in Mexico. Hancock Lee Jackson moved up to the office of chief executive from the lieutenant governorship. Following his inaugural, Governor Jackson called for a special election in August, and in October 1857 another new Governor was installed.

Robert Marcellus Stewart of St. Joseph was one of the most colorful chief executives of the pre-Civil War period. A bachelor, he was described by a contemporary as a "stranger to thrift but not to alcohol." A popular and capable Governor but an "eccentric statesman," he once pardoned all the women in the penitentiary and gave them employment at the executive residence where they "robbed and pillaged at their heart's content." One day he rode his horse up the front steps and into the house, ordering a servant to feed it a peck of oats. Accounts vary as to where the oats were served—from the piano, the Edwards sideboard or the fireplace mantel. The hoofprints remained on the wooden front steps for years.

"Governor Bob," as he was popularly known, constantly prodded the legislature for funds for a new official residence. His niece, Elizabeth Westcott Severance, was not impressed with the house when she arrived from New York to be his official hostess, but a redeeming feature was her uncle's collection of "exquisitely choice" plants on the two galleries. Before leaving in January 1861, Stewart again appealed to the legislature for the construction of a new mansion because the present one was so dilapidated it was virtually uninhabitable. Two months later bills were passed appropriating $20,000 for the construction of a new house, but before the money could be spent, the Civil War erupted. Missouri, along with the rest of the country, was plunged into a period of turbulence and bloodshed.

Claiborne Fox Jackson succeeded Robert Stewart. Jackson had the distinction of marrying successively three daughters of Dr. John Sappington, the quinine pioneer. The first Sappington daughter died five months after the wedding, the second died in an accident five years after her marriage. When Jackson returned to Arrow Rock to ask for the hand of yet another daughter, Dr. Sappington supposedly said, "You can take her, but don't come back after the old woman."

A Southern sympathizer, Jackson left Jefferson City in June 1861, one step ahead of Federal troops sent to occupy the capital. Seeking aid for the Confederacy, he first traveled to Texas and then Arkansas where he died the following year. His wife, too, had fled the capital, taking her family to exile in Texas where she died in 1864, "a refugee from the home of her youth and the grave of her father."

A special state convention declared the offices of Governor and Lieutenant Governor vacant and elected Hamilton Gamble, a former member of the Missouri Supreme Court, as provisional Governor. A Unionist, Gamble was instrumental in keeping Missouri from seceding. Upon his death in 1864, the provisional Lieutenant Governor, Willard Preble Hall, became Governor.

Life during the war years was dangerous and difficult. Guerillas and bushwhackers roamed the countryside, burning and looting. Confederate armies based in Arkansas launched periodic invasions in an attempt to win Missouri for the Confederacy. The last of these invasions was led by former Governor Sterling Price. Accompanying him was Thomas Caute Reynolds, Confederate Governor-in-Exile of Missouri, who had assumed the post after the death of Claiborne Jackson in 1862. Price's raid into Missouri in the autumn of 1864 was Reynolds' last chance to establish a Confederate stewardship of the state. The general took his troops to the outskirts of Jefferson City. For three days in early October, he was poised to launch an attack, hesitating, some said, because of the fond memories he had of the city during his governorship. Instead, pursued and harassed by Union cavalry, he marched to Westport, near the Kansas border. There, in a battle lasting several days, Union troops shattered his army and sent it straggling south to the safety of Arkansas and the Indian territories. Among the prisoners taken after Westport was Confederate Major General John S. Marmaduke of the Marmaduke-Sappington line, a future Missouri Governor.

Thomas C. Fletcher became Governor in January 1865, the first Republican to serve in that capacity in the history of the state. The Radical Republicans had emerged from the war politically victorious. Under the terms of the Drake Amendment (1865) Southerners who fought against the Union or expressed open sympathy for the Confederate cause were turned out of office and denied the right to vote—an act of vengeance that set back Reconstruction in Missouri for nearly a generation. The Drake Amendment also established a two-year term for the chief executive, a law which remained in effect until a new state constitution was written in 1875.

Governor Fletcher's family was the first to live in the executive residence since the administration of Sterling Price. He and his wife, Mary Clarissa, were betrothed in infancy and were married when they were 24 years old. Their daughter Frances Ella, an acknowledged beauty, was later the "reigning belle of St. Louis." A former officer in the Union Army and a friend of President Lincoln, Fletcher oversaw the passage three months before Appomattox of an emancipation ordinance making Missouri the first slave state to renounce the "peculiar institution."

Another Radical Republican, Joseph W. McClurg, followed Fletcher into office in 1869. A partisan of woman's suffrage, he also was an avowed prohibitionist, supporting a bill, which was resoundingly defeated, to bar the sale of intoxicants throughout the state. His hostess was his daughter, Frances Ann, a lively and intelligent girl who had been with her widowed father in Washington during his third term in Congress. In the years following the Civil War, Governors Fletcher and McClurg both had appealed in vain to the legislature for a new residence.

In 1871 Jefferson City was a thriving town of 5,000 people. Because of a sizable German population, breweries were a major industry. Progress had come in the form of coal-oil lamps perched atop wooden poles, illuminating the streets at night. A journey by railroad to St. Louis took only six to seven hours. Hogs and cows still roamed the streets, a situation the local newspaper called a "positive disgrace."

Disgraceful, too, was the Governor's aging residence. In 1868 an editorial declared, "That old rookery, known as the Governor's mansion, presents such a slushy appearance that a gentleman mistook it for a soap and candle manufactory a few days since."

B. Gratz Brown took office in January 1871. On February 10 a reception was held in the old house which many city residents declined to attend, fearing a disaster might result from overcrowding on the upper floors. This embarrassment finally spurred the legislature to action. On March 18 a bill was passed appropriating $50,000 for a new Executive Mansion to be constructed on the same location where the first residence/capitol had been built nearly 50 years before.

Proposals were solicited from various architects, and a plan submitted by the St. Louis firm of Barnett and Piquenard was accepted. The principal architect of the Mansion was George Ingham Barnett. Born in Nottingham, England, Barnett came to America in 1839 at the age of 24. After brief employment in New York, he journeyed west to St. Louis where he established a practice of his own. Before working with Piquenard, Barnett had designed the Union Methodist Church (1853) and the Chamber of Commerce Building (1857), both in St. Louis, as well as the elegant home of Ferdinand Kennett which overlooked the Mississippi River in Jefferson County. Those who commissioned Barnett were among the most prominent

Mansion architect George Ingham Barnett, portrait by Chester Harding.

21

citizens of St. Louis. Perhaps the most influential was Henry Shaw, a close friend and business associate. In addition to Shaw's commercial properties, Barnett designed his town house and country home, Tower Grove, located on the grounds of the present Missouri Botanical Gardens which was originally Shaw's country estate. His brief collaboration with Piquenard resulted in several houses, including the Blair-Huse Mansion on Lafayette Square in St. Louis, which featured distinctive mansard roofs.

Barnett was described as a man of great refinement and learning and a devotee of the classical school of architecture. A contemporary account declared that "he had no use for modern innovations and style, such as low ceilings, small windows and dwarfed door-ways. His buildings, whether public or private, always showed in their treatment what is characteristic of the educated architect, namely character, expression and proportion."

In May 1871 the construction contract was awarded to Gottlieb Martin of Jefferson City, who bid $56,500. Compared to other bids, the amount was high, but Martin had just completed a Jefferson City public school with a mansard roof similar to that of the proposed Mansion. The alley dividing the plot of land was closed, and while the old house was being razed, the new one, located on the north half of the plot, was being built.

On the next-to-last day of the year the new Mansion was completed. Governor Brown and his family did not move in until January 20, 1872. Three days later the first official function was held—a luncheon for Grand Duke Alexis of Russia who was on a hunting expedition to the West—and on the following evening, the grand ball. The new Mansion the guests thronged to see that night was a handsome Renaissance Revival building with Italianate and French influences, an architectural style also known as Second Empire.

The three-story structure of red brick with dressed stone blocks inlaid at the corners and under the window sills and door frames was crowned with an elegant sloping 13-foot mansard roof crested with delicate grillwork. The building was 66 feet, 6 inches square and faced east toward Madison Street. A side yard stretched 200 feet south to Capitol Avenue. The front portico was supported by four pink granite columns donated by Governor Brown from his own quarry in Iron County. (Brown's gift began the custom of First Families presenting a lasting memento to the Mansion.) Unfortunately, when the columns arrived, they were nine inches too short and a second base had to be added to make them fit.

The front entrance featured the hand-carved double walnut doors, which were 14 feet high. The first floor rooms—the Great Hall, Library, Double Parlor and Dining Room—were designed to accommodate guests. Perhaps the most splendid feature was the Grand Stairway with a railing hand-carved from walnut by a Swiss artisan from Carthage. It was (and is) considered one of the most beautiful free-flowing stairways in the country.

The second floor contained seven bedrooms opening off a large stair hall; the third floor, six bedrooms and a ballroom also used as a "supper room" and billiard hall. A steep and narrow back stair was the only access to the third floor, an arduous climb for

Victorian ladies in billowing gowns and waiters bearing heavy trays. In the basement was the kitchen, laundry, storeroom, boiler and a dumbwaiter for serving the upper floors. The final cost of the building, including some furnishings, was $74,960.

Two weeks after the gala reception, Governor Brown and his wife began a hectic schedule of state social affairs. The custom of entertaining legislators at small dinner parties, suspended during the Civil War, was revived. On one occasion Gratz K. Brown, the Governor's 10-year-old son, sawed several chair legs short with a set of carpentry tools presented to him by his father. The deed went undiscovered until the guests sat down to dinner and began tilting and listing in all directions.

Silas Woodson, the first Democrat elected Governor after the Civil War, succeeded B. Gratz Brown in office. Woodson was 53; his wife, Jennie, was 26, the youngest First Lady in the history of the state. An energetic, vivacious woman, Jennie Woodson gave many dances and masquerade balls. Characteristic of Victorian hospitality, the Woodsons shared the Mansion with several of their relatives. During their two-year (1873-1875) occupancy, twin daughters were born to Jennie's sister and brother-in-law, the first births in an executive residence since 1856, and the first wedding was held, that of Jennie's sister-in-law, Cornelia Shannon, and William Newton White of Columbia.

The administration of Charles H. Hardin, in entertainment style at least, offered a distinct contrast to Silas Woodson's. Mary Barr Hardin was an austere First Lady, a Greek and Latin scholar and a devout Baptist. At the outset of his term, Governor Hardin announced that there would be no masquerade balls at the Mansion. At his wife's urging, a special day of fasting and prayer was held on June 3, 1875, at the height of a grasshopper plague that was destroying Missouri's crops; the next day rain fell, and shortly thereafter the grasshoppers disappeared. That same year the capital city welcomed two important if rather different guests: King Kalakaua of the Sandwich Islands (Hawaii) and Jefferson Davis, former President of the Confederate States of America.

John S. Phelps, a strong Union Democrat, was elected Governor in 1877 and served the first four-year term since the 1850s. His wife, Mary Whitney Phelps, was a remarkable woman who had been widely praised for her activities during the Civil War. She served as a nurse at the bloody battle of Pea Ridge, Arkansas, in March 1862; afterward, she opened an orphanage in Springfield for children of the slain Union and Confederate soldiers. She died in 1878, and her daughter, Mrs. Mary Phelps Montgomery, acted as the Governor's official hostess. Governor Phelps was a lavish entertainer, and at his inaugural dinner a sumptuous feast was served that included 20 ornamented cakes and ice creams of a dozen delicate flavors molded into swans, dolphins and bouquets of flowers. Mrs. Montgomery's son was the first grandson of a Governor to be born in the Mansion.

The bitterness of the Civil War years was slowly subsiding as postwar prosperity accelerated. It was the age of high Victorian splendor and extravagant taste. The young Republic was nearing the end of its first century of development.

The Executive Mansion, a decade old, was a symbol of unity for a state strongly divided during the war. It was a place to which all Missourians, staunch Unionist and embittered Secessionist, could point with pride.

But echoes of the turbulent war years were still being heard across the state. In the 1870s, primarily because of the exploits of the James-Younger gang, Missouri had acquired a nationwide reputation as the "Outlaw State." In 1882 Governor Thomas T. Crittenden offered a reward for the capture and conviction of the bandits, particularly Frank and Jesse James. Crittenden's offer of a reward sent search parties looking for the Jameses. It also brought threats against the Governor and his family from those to whom the outlaws represented the last breath of Southern sentiment or a bold defiance of large eastern corporations, especially the railroads.

On April 3, 1882, Jesse James was killed in St. Joseph. Frank James remained in hiding for several months, finally surrendering in Jefferson City in October 1882. News of the surrender spread swiftly through the town. McCarty's Hotel, where James was staying, held an open house and the public flocked there to see the country's most famous living bandit.

During the Crittenden administration, the Mansion exterior received the first of many coats of red paint when the legislature responded to the Governor's appeal to remedy the soot-"blackened and stained condition of the outside."

In 1882 tragedy struck the Crittenden family. Carrie Crittenden, age 9, the Governor's only daughter, died of diphtheria in

December. Earlier that year, with the threats pouring into the Mansion, she had been faithfully guarded by David Glenn, a retainer in the Crittenden household. Carrie's last words were, "Drive on, David, I see the angels." Her death was the first to occur in the new Mansion and her funeral, sadly, was held there amidst the festive Christmas decorations. To honor her memory, the family donated an ornate walnut bedroom suite to be used in the house.

John S. Marmaduke was the first officer of the Confederacy to be elected Governor of Missouri, a sign that the hostilities of the war years were finally easing. A West Point graduate, he had been an officer in the United States Army, and after choosing the cause of the South he served with distinction in the Confederate Army during the Civil War, attaining the rank of Major General. He fought at the Battle of Westport (October 1864), and later was captured by Union troops in an engagement at Mine Creek, Kansas.

Marmaduke was the fourth bachelor to serve as Missouri's Governor, and the first to live in the new Mansion. His election in 1885 marked the pinnacle of the Sappington-Marmaduke dynasty. He was a popular Governor, and serving as his official hostesses were his two nieces, Lalla Marmaduke Nelson and Iola Harwood. Governor Marmaduke liked fresh air, and he used the Great Hall of the Mansion as an office. In cold weather, when the heavy walnut doors were closed, it was too dark to work; his solution was to add glass doors to the front entrance. The highlight of his social season was the annual Christmas party for children, presided over by his nieces. It was on the eve of the third of these, in December 1887,

that the Governor died of pneumonia. He was the first chief executive to die in the Mansion.

Lieutenant Governor Albert P. Morehouse succeeded Marmaduke in office and served until 1889. Following the four-month period of mourning, First Lady Martha McFadden Morehouse adopted a popular custom and gave as her first entertainment a "Pink Reception," with decorations and refreshments planned around a single color.

In the late 1880s the Jefferson City population reached 8,000, almost evenly divided between German immigrants and native-born Americans. Electricity arrived in 1887, and a year later a light was shining on the Mansion's front lawn. Additional progress was achieved in May 1888 when a city ordinance was passed which prohibited livestock from roaming the streets. In the next decade a new bridge funded by the citizens of the capital city was built across the Missouri River, linking Jefferson City with agriculture and commerce in the northern half of the state. Another major achievement by local residents was the successful campaign to keep the capital in Jefferson City—after years of discussion about moving the capital to Sedalia because of its easier accessibility.

The first extensive renovation of the Mansion took place during the administration of David Rowland Francis (1889-1893). The Missouri legislature appropriated $11,000 for repairs, and while workers invaded the house, the First Lady, Jane Perry Francis, and her children moved back to their home in St. Louis. The exterior walls of the Mansion "received a new coat of deep red paint" to cover soot stains, and the rooms on each floor were refurbished with new paint, wallpaper and furniture. The plumbing facilities were connected to the new city water system and electricity was installed, as well as a new steam-heating system. Structurally, Mrs. Francis added two small windows in the wall at the end of the Nook, a sitting area under the Grand Stairway. Not only did Mrs. Francis facilitate the renovation of the Executive Mansion, but she also was effective in convincing legislators that the University of Missouri should remain in Columbia after the disastrous fire in January 1892 that destroyed Academic Hall.

David Francis was a former Mayor of St. Louis, and the Francises were accustomed to entertaining. They held the first Inaugural Ball in the Mansion since the Phelps administration. A strong intelligent woman, Mrs. Francis typified a growing post-Civil War development of the influential First Lady, a woman of character and refinement, capable of exerting a positive influence upon state policy. Mrs. Francis might be regarded as a transitional figure—a woman of Victorian rectitude, endowed with an assertive temperament, who was not afraid of expressing her opinions.

During the William Joel Stone administration (1893-1897), a water pipe in the Dining Room ceiling burst just before a formal dinner party. Sarah Stone calmly directed the servants to move the tables and chairs to a drier part of the room and dinner was served on time. It was not surprising that soon after the incident the legislature again approved an appropriation to repair faulty plumbing. The bill also included funds to build new stables. The Stones began the tradition of the New Year's Day Military Ball.

Lon Vest Stephens, Governor at the turn of the century (1897-1901), and his wife, Margaret, were a wealthy couple from Cooper County whose social style reflected the high fashion of the Gay Nineties. Their private income helped supplement the cost of entertainment at the Mansion. The cost of the second major Mansion renovation was funded by a $7,000 appropriation from the legislature in 1897. A portion of the appropriation was used for new china, and the rest for the acquisition of dark rich fabrics and furniture. The First Empire theme was generally followed in the selection of wallpaper, draperies and furnishings. The Library walls were covered with tapestry of royal purple and gold, and draperies of heavy gold French velour hung at the windows. English oak furniture was upholstered in Morocco-stamped leather. In contrast to the deep tones used in the Library, the Great Hall was finished in rich shades of rose, coral and ivory. The Double Parlor woodwork was painted ivory and the furniture and drapery fabric was rose-pink damask. French wallpaper was used in the Dining Room. Rugs throughout the first floor rooms were green with a design of deep pink rosebuds. The upstairs bedrooms also were redecorated, and a fountain was installed on the Mansion grounds. Lavish and sumptuous, the décor of the Mansion during the Stephens era typified the flamboyant taste of the *fin-de-siècle* period.

Highlighting the 1898 social season at the Mansion was the performance of a light opera followed by a buffet supper. Special invitations were issued, and the dessert table featured a harp made of flowers and cakes baked in the shapes of musical instruments.

*Executive Mansion
exterior prior to 1900
with its brick painted red.*

Double Parlor, 20th anniversary party of Governor and Mrs. Lon Vest Stephens, October, 1900.

The next year at a *bal masque,* Governor Stephens wore a "plaid costume with a red stovepipe hat and carried a china pug dog. Mrs. Stephens appeared as a Gibson Military Girl wearing a red velvet coat, a sword and a cocked hat with a feather." The most elaborate party during the Stephens administration was their twentieth anniversary celebration on October 5, 1900. Mrs. Stephens selected her dress for the evening from her wardrobe of Paris gowns.

Mrs. Stephens was responsible for originating a Mansion tradition—the oil portrait of the First Lady. Financed by women throughout the state, the portrait was painted by J. W. Cunningham, a St. Louis artist. While posing, Mrs. Stephens read a popular novel of the day, *When Knighthood Was in Flower.*

The melancholy of the Alexander Dockery administration (1901-1905) was a contrast to the gaiety of its predecessor. In the years before their occupancy of the Mansion, all of the Dockerys' eight children had died. In addition, Mrs. Dockery suffered a heart condition and social events had to be reduced in size. Despite her afflictions, Mary Dockery was a keen observer of politics. When her husband was a Missouri representative in Congress, she regularly read every newspaper in his district and kept him informed of the opinions of his constituents.

On January 1, 1903—the day of the Military Ball— Mrs. Dockery died of heart failure. She was the first wife of a chief executive to die in the Mansion. The funeral was held beneath the bunting and other decorations for the Ball.

Kate Morrow, wife of the executive clerk, was asked

by the Governor to assist him as Missouri's official hostess. In 1903 she supervised the construction of the first major structural addition to the Mansion, a porte-cochère on the south side. The addition provided a sheltered entrance for guests and reduced the drafts in the Great Hall. The new south entrance opened on a hall and back stairway to the second floor where guests could leave their wraps and then descend the Grand Stairway.

Official entertaining increased for the widowed Governor in 1904 when the Louisiana Purchase Exposition opened in St. Louis. Former Governor David Francis served as president of the World's Fair. In June of the same year the Mansion was the scene for the wedding reception of Mildred Stone, daughter of the former Governor.

At 35 Joseph Folk became one of the youngest Governors in Missouri history. Unlike her predecessors, Gertrude Folk, 32, took no interest in politics, refusing even to be photographed during her husband's campaign. During the first year of their administration (1905), disaster was narrowly averted when a fire started in the Great Hall fireplace chimney and spread upstairs to the second-floor bedrooms. Fortunately, the Governor was working late. He ran from his office and threw 100 tubes of firedust, a dry-powder extinguisher, on the blaze, which checked it until firemen arrived. The damage was $4,000 to the building and $11,000 to the carpets and furniture. Insurance money and $18,000 from the legislature enabled Gertrude Folk to redecorate the Mansion. The Great Hall marble fireplace mantel was replaced with the present one of solid black

Children of Governor and Mrs. Hadley playing on the fountain installed during the Stephens administration.

walnut. Gold-leafed furniture formerly used at the Missouri Pavilion of the St. Louis World's Fair was repaired and later placed in the parlor. Tapestry wall coverings were added to the Dining Room.

Herbert Hadley and his wife, Agnes, also were in their 30s when they moved into the Mansion in 1909. They brought their three young children, a lively group who played an occasional game of football in the Great Hall. A tutor was employed to teach classes in an improvised schoolroom on the third floor. Later, a dancing instructor was engaged to teach the youngsters waltzes and two-steps and proper party manners.

Governor Hadley was a congenial host and enjoyed having guests at his table. An avid sportsman, he participated in an annual autumn hunt in the woods outside Jefferson City. One year the hunt resulted in a bountiful banquet at the Mansion; the menu included roast quail, roast wild turkey, roast possum, roast coon, fried rabbit, squirrel stew, roast saddle of venison, roast wild duck, creamed potatoes, turnips, peas, fruit salad, pumpkin pie, cheese, nuts and coffee.

On Sunday, February 5, 1911, lightning struck the dome of the capitol, starting a fire that completely destroyed the building. For the second time, an irreplaceable archive of historical documents, including early records of the Executive Mansion and seven portraits by George Caleb Bingham, went up in flames. Fortunately, the Mansion was some distance from the capitol and was never in danger. While her husband helped fight the fire, Mrs. Hadley wrapped her children in blankets and sat them in the deep window

February 11, 1911 fire which destroyed the capitol and the state's treasury of official documents.

Mansion exterior showing the porte-cochère (1904) and the second-floor porch added during the Major administration.

sills on the west side of the Mansion to watch the venerable old capitol burn.

Construction began on the new Capitol during the administration of Elliott W. Major (1913-1917). Henry Hope Reed and Christopher Tunnard in their book *American Skyline* called it "perhaps the most Roman of all [state capitols] in scale and character." At the top of the dome, 260 feet from the ground, is the figure of Ceres, goddess of fertility of the land, an appropriate symbol for an agricultural state. On the walls of the House Lounge, Thomas Hart Benton in 1936 painted his famous murals depicting Missouri history.

Important additions also were made to the Mansion at this time. A second-floor screened porch was added above an already existing first-floor porch at the back of the house. Electric lights were installed along the driveway which was graded and resurfaced.

The inauguration of Frederick Gardner in 1917 took place on the south steps of the new Capitol, a tradition that has been maintained through the years. During the Inaugural Ball, champagne was served by mistake although the Governor had declared that there would be no liquor at official Mansion functions. A gift of champagne had been delivered with bottles of sparkling grape juice and was served accidentally during the inaugural festivities.

In April of that year the United States declared war on Germany. First Lady Jeannette Vosburgh Gardner became very involved in the war effort, planting the state's first "war garden" on the

Mansion grounds and volunteering regularly for Red Cross work. Her son was one of 25 University of Missouri students who organized an American Field Service unit which served in France. Armistice was declared November 11, 1918.

Two important postwar issues occupied the attention of Governor Gardner. In April 1919 he signed a bill which permitted women in Missouri to vote for President for the first time. Earlier, he presided over the state's ratification of the Eighteenth Amendment which forbade the purchase and consumption of alcoholic beverages. Fearful of "finishing his time . . . in a bone-dry world," a prison employee pocketed a bottle of Mrs. Gardner's best perfume and a bottle of the Governor's hair tonic and disappeared. He was found later "very drunk and very sick."

Few changes were made at the Mansion during the Gardner administration, but a small playhouse was built on the river terrace below the Dining Room porch for the Gardners' 8-year-old daughter, Janet.

In 1921 the Mansion celebrated its fiftieth year, and much had changed over the past half-century. More automobiles than horse-drawn vehicles could be found on the streets of Jefferson City, and inside the Mansion electric lights, rather than oil lamps or gas lights, illuminated the rooms. The new decade ushered in the era of the flapper, and at the Inaugural Ball Mrs. Arthur M. Hyde wore a modishly "modern" ankle-length dress of metallic cloth with a lace overdress that hung straight from the shoulders. The poor health of the First Lady, aggravated by an injury in an automobile accident,

New State Capitol,
dedicated October 6, 1924.

precluded a heavy schedule of entertaining. The formal dedication of the new State Capitol took place on October 6, 1924 and thousands thronged to Jefferson City to participate in the dedication and watch (in the rain) the pageant dramatizing Missouri's history.

Arthur Hyde, a conservative Republican, paid the Mansion food bills out of his own pocket. Help was forthcoming from the Missouri legislature for more substantial household expenses (a total of $43,000 between 1921 and 1925) such as recarpeting, rewiring and the purchase of a Steinway grand piano.

Significant changes in the social activities at the Mansion took place during the administration of Sam A. Baker (1925-1929). The executive residence could no longer be the exclusive site of official social functions because of the tremendous crowds. For the first time in Missouri history, the Inaugural Ball was held in the Capitol rotunda. The Mansion's ballroom would no longer accommodate the state balls, but periodic dinners for legislators as well as teas and socials still were held on the lower floors. Additionally, two weddings involving family friends were held in the Mansion during the Baker years.

In June of 1927 the First Family joined other proud Missourians in St. Louis for an official welcome to Charles A. Lindbergh, who had just returned after making his memorable solo flight to Paris in "The Spirit of St. Louis." Governor Baker himself had traveled briefly in an airplane and later his daughter, Mary Elisabeth, flew from St. Louis to Jefferson City in 55 minutes—a record time—in a plane piloted by the chief of the Air Corps of Missouri. Compared to the early days of railroading and the even earlier days when the journey to St. Louis was by horse or keelboat, the trip was a milestone.

Improved roads and advances in transportation brought more dignitaries to the Mansion and increased the duties and responsibilities of Missouri's First Ladies. Women had become an important political factor by the 1930s and the wife of a Governor could contribute significantly to the success of her husband's administration.

Henry S. Caulfield's inauguration in 1929, the first to be broadcast over radio, was held at the Capitol, where all the inaugural festivities including the Governor's reception were moved because of the deteriorating condition of the Mansion (the Grand Stairway was considered unsafe for crowds). Extensive repairs could not be made but funds were appropriated for improvements including an electric range and refrigerator for the basement kitchen and flower gardens with a stepping-stone walk that led down the face of the terraced bluff.

The First Lady, the former Frances Delano, was a distant relative of Franklin and Eleanor Roosevelt. Mrs. Caulfield was the first candidate's wife to accompany her husband on campaign trips. During her husband's term, she published a series of articles in the *Missouri Ruralist* that offered an intimate look into behind-the-scenes life at the Mansion. Charles F. Galt was commissioned to paint Mrs. Caulfield's official portrait in which she was shown wearing a

Mrs. Guy Park entertains former First Ladies Mrs. Caulfield, Mrs. Hyde and Mrs. Hadley at a tea in 1934.

fashionable short gown. Later, when hemlines dropped, Mr. Galt was asked to return and repaint the gown so it covered her knees.

The lean years of the Great Depression forced the legislature to cut back drastically on Mansion appropriations; the total budget for the first two years (1933-1935) of the Guy B. Park administration was $14,500. Despite the limited funds, First Lady Eleanora Gabbert Park managed to buy curtains, window shades and china and keep up the required painting and repairs as well as continue official entertaining. A highlight of their years at the Mansion was the wedding of Henrietta Park on November 16, 1933—the Parks' twenty-fourth wedding anniversary. The wedding was the first of the daughter of a Governor in office in nearly a hundred years. Interested in the history of the Mansion, Mrs. Park and Kate Morrow, hostess for Governor Dockery (1901-1905), published a book entitled *Women of the Mansion* (1936), a unique compendium of Mansion customs and traditions.

The economic realities of the Depression had derailed a movement to raze and replace the Mansion, but it still was in pathetic physical condition. During the first winter of their tenure, the Lloyd C. Starks (1937-1941) had to stuff rags in the windows to keep out the cold and place buckets under holes in the leaky roof to catch the rain. The rat-infested basement kitchen flooded periodically and the small, slow dumbwaiter from the kitchen was inadequate for large dinners. Most crucial was the state of the Grand Stairway which sagged dangerously away from the wall. State architect Raymond L. Voskamp estimated the cost of repairs and new furnishings at $55,000.

Wedding photograph of Henrietta Park Krause, daughter of Governor and Mrs. Guy Park, 1933.

Governor and Mrs. Lloyd C. Stark and their two daughters descending the Grand Stairway following the renovation.

The legislature approved funding, and with the help of a St. Louis decorator supervised by Mrs. Stark, Voskamp began extensive renovation.

The mother of two children, Katherine Stark made a home for them and maintained a lively social schedule while workmen were everywhere. It was not uncommon for Mansion help serving meals to have to work around piles of equipment or scaffolding. The list of changes achieved by this fourth major renovation of the Mansion is impressive. The porte-cochère was replaced with a two-story wing containing a new kitchen on the first floor and garages below. The dumbwaiter was removed and a serving pantry added in its place. Steel brackets were inserted to secure the Grand Stairway to the wall without having to resort to unsightly columns for support. Heating pipes were concealed in the walls and new wiring and telephones were added. Parquet floors were laid in the Great Hall and new carpets covered the floors. The downstairs walls were stripped of several layers of wallpaper, covered with canvas and repainted. The exterior of the Mansion was painted white for the first time and a new roof was installed. The grounds were relandscaped, and the Starks donated 3,000 new plantings for the project from their nursery in Louisiana, Missouri.

A contested election between boss-dominated Democrats and reform-minded Republicans delayed the inauguration of Forrest C. Donnell until late February 1941. Ten months later Japan attacked Pearl Harbor, and for the second time in an already turbulent century, the United States was at war. Activity was sharply curtailed by food and fuel shortages. The lights illuminating the dome on the Capitol were extinguished and the Governor asked Missourians to observe a voluntary 35 mile-an-hour speed limit to conserve rubber. First Lady Hilda Hays Donnell was involved in many war-time activities and invited servicemen to holiday festivities at the Mansion. An addition to the grounds given by the Donnells was a hitching post initialed "JCD" (for the Governor's father) from the Governor's boyhood home in Maryville.

Former Governor and Mrs. Caulfield at the Inaugural Reception, 1941, of Governor and Mrs. Forrest Donnell in the Mansion Dining Room.

Shortages continued to be an inconvenience during the administration of Phil M. Donnelly (1945-1949). A friend made Juanita Donnelly's inaugural gown from a length of green satin on which Mrs. Donnelly herself beaded a design in pearls at the neckline and waistband. Help was difficult to obtain since the labor force was either in the service or working in a war industry.

The news of the Japanese surrender aboard the *U.S.S. Missouri* on September 2, 1945 was greeted with elation.

While the Donnellys were in residence, the tapestry which had covered the Dining Room walls for 40 years was removed; the tapestry adhesive had served as a breeding ground for moths and had plagued First Ladies for decades. Mrs. Donnelly's completion of the Governor's Garden between the Mansion and the Capitol is a lasting memorial.

Forrest Smith and his wife, Mildred, celebrated twice in January 1949—their formal investiture as Governor and First Lady of Missouri and the inauguration of Harry S. Truman as President of the United States. A special train transported home-state friends to Washington for the festivities on January 20, just 10 days after the new Governor had been inaugurated. The Governor's annual goose-hunting trip once yielded the main course for an "all-states" Christmas dinner featuring gifts from Governors of other states—citrus fruit from Texas, potatoes from Maine, sweet potatoes from Louisiana, celery from Colorado and the Missouri goose.

In June 1950 the Korean conflict began. Appropriations were again curtailed, but under Mrs. Smith's guiding hand the Mansion exterior was repainted after an unsuccessful attempt at sandblasting. A new porch cornice was added, new steam lines were introduced and the first automatic dishwasher was installed, an invaluable aid to the limited Mansion staff.

Phil Donnelly returned to office in 1953, making him the first Missouri Governor to be re-elected to a second four-year term. As Donnelly returned, another valued state servant departed: Barbara Pohlman retired. She was the housekeeper upon whom so many First Families had depended since 1909.

The 1953 assessed valuation of the Mansion was $242,000—$179,000 for the building and grounds, and $63,000 for furniture. Irritated with the chronic high cost of Mansion upkeep, many legislators were eager to house future First Families in a more modest and efficient home. To the relief of the preservationists, Governor Donnelly vetoed a $250,000 appropriation for a new residence.

Governor and Mrs. Donnelly and Lieutenant Governor and Mrs. Blair leading the Inaugural Grand March in the Capitol Rotunda, 1953.

At the close of her stewardship as First Lady, Mrs. Donnelly suggested that a committee be appointed to be permanent custodian of the building so that each First Lady would have assistance in this area. The advice was not heeded.

Two days after his inauguration, Governor James T. Blair remarked to a gathering of friends that he had no intention of living in the Mansion. His list of complaints against the old house was long and eloquent. The basement was infested with rats, the woodwork riddled with worms, the plumbing antiquated and the wallpaper in shambles. The Grand Stairway, with its 36 steps, he named Cardiac Hill.

The Governor and his wife, Emilie, spent their inaugural night in the Mansion, returning the next day to their home in Jefferson City where they had lived for 25 years. In response to the furor created by his remarks, Blair announced that he would hold all traditional public functions in the Mansion, but that the fate of the structure as the official home of Missouri's chief executives would rest with the legislature.

The Governor's actions renewed the enthusiasm of legislators for having the Mansion razed—one proposal was to turn the grounds into a parking lot. However, a committee of architects and construction experts was appointed and found that although the interior definitely was in need of renovation, the Mansion was structurally sound. The committee recommended that the Mansion be completely restored to its original appearance at an estimated cost of $500,000. In response, the legislature voted $40,000 for repairs only.

With this modest sum, several major improvements were made. An elevator was installed, two bedrooms and a sitting room on the second floor were air-conditioned, refurbished and redecorated, and a small kitchen for the private use of the executive family was built into a storage closet on the second floor. New decorations and carpeting were introduced throughout the house and several structural repairs were completed. The Blairs moved into the partially rehabilitated house in October 1958. In February of the following year their son was married in the Great Hall—the first Mansion wedding of a Governor's son.

Renovation, including extensive redecoration of the first floor, continued during the administration of John Dalton (1961-1965). Geraldine Dalton enjoyed entertaining, and while she was First Lady, 13,876 people sat down to meals at the Mansion—an average of nine a day! Mrs. Dalton also originated the tradition of the Easter Egg Roll for handicapped children, which was held on the Mansion grounds. Mrs. Dalton loved the old house and encouraged people to visit it. Entrance through the huge walnut doors she called a "handclasp with history," a handclasp that extended far afield when she conducted a televised tour of the Mansion. The efforts of this remarkable woman helped to upgrade the image of the house in the public eye. Like Mrs. Donnelly, Mrs. Dalton wanted to establish a program that would provide continuity and order to the planning and maintenance program of the Mansion. Although her efforts were rebuffed by the legislature, they foreshadowed the establishment of a group such as Missouri Mansion Preservation, Incorporated.

Detail of carved medallion of massive walnut front doors.

When Warren and Betty Hearnes moved into the Mansion in 1965 they brought three young daughters—Lynne, Leigh and Julie B.—the first children to reside in the Mansion since the Lloyd Starks' family in the 1930s. The third floor was converted into their living area and the elevator that Governor Blair had taken to the second floor to avoid the steps of Cardiac Hill was extended to permit the girls to ride directly to their quarters from the lower level. A menagerie of pets became beguiling third-floor residents, and a trampoline was an exciting addition to the play area.

A constitutional amendment enabled Warren Hearnes to become the first Governor in Missouri history to be re-elected to a second consecutive four-year term. During these years (1969-1973) Betty Hearnes devoted her energies to renovating the exterior of the Mansion. The most difficult and time-consuming job was the removal of numerous layers of paint that had coated the exterior since the late nineteenth century. A less harmful method than sandblasting was employed by first applying chemicals to the old brick, then washing the solution off with high-pressure water hoses. It took seven months to complete the entire exterior, nearly as long as it took to build the Mansion in 1871. The mansard roof was reshingled with dark slate and the decorative iron grillwork cresting the roof was cleaned and repaired.

In addition to exterior restoration, Mrs. Hearnes uncovered the parquet floor in the Great Hall and freed the shutters from their pockets in the window casings where they had been nailed in place prior to the turn of the century. Mrs. Hearnes also replaced the huge sliding pocket doors between the Great Hall and the Dining Room with reproductions of the originals. The first- and second-story porches at the back of the Mansion were glazed, which provided a sheltered retreat for the First Family and a year-round view of the Capitol and the Missouri River. The number of tours by appointment, begun by Mrs. Donnelly and continued by other First Ladies, increased during the Hearnes administration.

Christopher Samuel Bond, the youngest Governor in Missouri history, took office in January 1973 at 33. His wife, Carolyn Reid Bond, a native Kentuckian, campaigned for her husband in each of Missouri's 114 counties. Her one campaign promise—to open the Executive Mansion to the public on a regular basis—was fulfilled in April 1973. In keeping that promise two new traditions, regularly scheduled public tours and Christmas Candlelight Tours, were born. Assisted by a group of volunteer tour guides, the Missouri Mansion Docents, the Bonds welcomed more than 150,000 visitors to the Mansion during their first term, most of them personally greeted by the First Lady.

Both Governor and Mrs. Bond brought to the Mansion a keen interest in historic preservation. Early in his term, the Governor was instrumental in saving the Wainwright Building in St. Louis, designed in 1891 by Louis Sullivan and considered one of the first architectural expressions of the modern skyscraper. A perfect candidate for adaptive reuse, the building underwent extensive exterior restoration and was converted into the St. Louis State Office Building.

Mrs. Bond played an important leadership role in the adoption of the state's official project to commemorate the country's bicentennial—restoration of Jefferson City's early steamboat landing and designation of the landmark as a State Historic Site. Located between the Executive Mansion and the Capitol, Jefferson Landing includes three restored structures: the Lohman Building, the Union Hotel and the Christopher Maus House. The site was officially dedicated by Governor and Mrs. Bond on July 4, 1976.

Another project commemorating the nation's anniversary was the creation of the Missouri Bicentennial Needlepoint Rug. Begun on July 4, 1974, the project took 18 months to complete and involved 81 needlepointers from across the state. The canvas was painted by two needlepoint designers from Mexico, Missouri. The 10 by 11-foot rug features the 49 state flowers encircled by a border of the Missouri state flower, the hawthorn blossom. Mrs. Bond stitched the Kentucky goldenrod, the flower of her native state. The rug's nearly 2,000,000 stitches represent more than 4,000 hours of volunteer work. Unveiled by the Bonds at the Mansion on January 30, 1976, the rug was donated to Missouri Mansion Preservation, Inc. at the end of the bicentennial year for its continued use at the Mansion.

Over the years a "crisis-correction" approach to maintenance had been com-

Second-floor historic Stark Bedroom featuring 1976 Bicentennial Needlepoint Rug.

monplace in caring for the Mansion. To protect and preserve a vital part of Missouri heritage for future generations, careful restoration and long-range planning were necessary. After more than a year of research and planning by Mrs. Bond, using the White House Fine Arts Committee as a primary example, she laid the foundation for the formation of Missouri Mansion Preservation, Inc. Through her efforts, supported by former First Ladies Mrs. Lloyd Stark and Mrs. John Dalton as well as First Family descendants and concerned individuals throughout the state, Missouri Mansion Preservation, Inc. (MMPI) was incorporated in October 1974. The statewide, nonpartisan, not-for-profit organization was composed of a 28-member Board of Directors, with all former Governors and First Ladies as honorary members. Dedicated to the restoration and historical interpretation of the Executive Mansion, MMPI also was designed to provide continuity in these programs from one administration to the next.

To provide the basis for a thorough restoration, it was important to select an architect sensitive to the historical character of the Mansion as well as to its dual function as a private home and public building. Theodore J. Wofford, A.I.A., of the St. Louis firm of Murphy, Downey, Wofford & Richman, was chosen as the restoration architect, and he immediately began exhaustive research on the Executive Mansion, George Ingham Barnett and the Italianate, Second Empire and Renaissance Revival periods. A thorough structural investigation was scheduled and measured drawings of the Mansion's four levels were completed. The results, published by MMPI in the 71-page *Missouri Executive Mansion: A Long Range Development Study*

(1975), included a brief history of the Mansion, a report on the structural components of the building and a recommendation for restoration on a phase-by-phase basis. Structural funds for the project were to be supplied by the legislature and antiques and period furnishings by MMPI through private funds and donations.

The underlying philosophy of the project was that of a "living restoration"—a restoration that was authentic to the 1871 period when the Mansion was built, yet adaptable to today's functions. Unlike those in a strict museum restoration, the restored public rooms would be intensively used. Because of documentation showing that Renaissance Revival furniture was purchased for the Mansion in 1871, this style was adopted as a unifying decorative form.

The Renaissance Revival style of furniture was first introduced to the United States at the New York Crystal Palace Exhibition in 1853. However, it was not until after the Civil War that the style was incorporated into decorating schemes, and it remained popular until around 1880. The Renaissance Revival style was based on the sixteenth-century European Renaissance, a period when art and architecture were governed by the principles of light, space, harmony and proportion. By the nineteenth century the Romantic Movement brought a renewed interest in eclecticism—the

Fine example of Renaissance Revival style in a period side cabinet located in the Great Hall.

Detail of window cornice stenciling in Library restoration.

borrowing of older styles to create new ones. Based on a striking conjunction of classical proportions and linear detail, Renaissance Revival style is massive in scale yet restrained in character. Architectural details, sculptural figures and symmetrical patterns provide a decorative effect, while the basic design remains simple and elegant.

Restoration of the Mansion Library was MMPI's first major project. Scarcity of original documentation prohibited a literal restoration. However, by using research available—and references to a green and gold color scheme, the use of elaborate window treatments and acquisition of the Renaissance Revival furniture—as well as comparative studies of other libraries of the period, a comprehensive restoration was achieved. Walnut, a native wood of Missouri, was a guide in furniture selection. A Renaissance Revival center table, a suite of five chairs, a secretary and bookcases were acquired for the Library, as well as a geometric-patterned Wilton carpet. The ceiling and cornice were accented by stenciling and gilt highlights. The window treatments, restating the stencil pattern in gold leaf and embroidery details, were adapted from the 1869 Governor's Mansion in Albany, New York. Window shutters were returned to their original light color, as documented by the earliest photograph, and hand-embroidered sheer curtains complemented the heavy gold over-curtains. As their official gift, Governor and Mrs. Bond donated the overmantel mirror, which is dated March 30, 1870.

While the project took two years of planning and fund raising, it took only six weeks to complete. On August 10, 1976, when Missouri celebrated 155 years of statehood, the Library was formally dedicated. Joining the Bonds for the dedication ceremony were White House Curator Clement Conger and Adrienna Scalamandré Bitter, consultant for the Library restoration and owner of Scalamandré, the New York firm known world-wide for its reproduction of documented fabrics, trims and carpet. Providing an impetus for the continuing restoration of the first floor was an announcement during the ceremony of a benefactor gift from Mr. and Mrs. James Smith McDonnell of St. Louis, through the McDonnell-Douglas Foundation, for the Great Hall restoration.

Following the example of First Lady Margaret Nelson Stephens at the turn of the century, friends of Mrs. Bond from across the state made small contributions for the painting of the First Lady's official portrait. Artist Gilbert Early of St. Louis was commissioned to complete the portrait, which was unveiled in the fall of 1976.

White House Curator Clement Conger with Governor and Mrs. Bond during 1976 Library restoration festivities.

Hospitality was an important part of the Bonds' life during their first administration. Records show that more than 70,000 people were entertained at the Mansion between 1973 and 1977. Among the guests were U.S. Secretary of State Henry Kissinger and his wife, Nancy, who joined the First Family in May 1975 for breakfast at the Mansion on the Bonds' eighth wedding anniversary. Old traditions like the Military Ball and the Easter Egg Roll were revived and long-standing customs like the Inaugural Reception, legislative dinners and the State Dinner were maintained. Music provided a special accent to the enter-

taining—from the rock band that played at the Mansion for the post-inaugural party and the Scott Joplin concert series to the Cantorum's Christmas carols during the Candlelight Tours.

Former Jackson County Prosecutor Joseph P. Teasdale was elected Governor in 1976. During his years at the Mansion the size of his family increased when he and his wife, Theresa, adopted a son, John, in 1978, who joined their two-year-old son, Billy. In 1979 Mrs. Teasdale gave birth to another son, Kevin.

In addition to her dedication to her children, Mrs. Teasdale pursued her interests in gardening and animals. She stabled her horse near Jefferson City and enjoyed exercising her dogs on the Mansion grounds.

The new Governor and First Lady continued the traditions of regular public tours and the annual Christmas Candlelight Tours. Additionally, several structural repairs outlined in the Long Range Development Study were accomplished including renovation of the backstair area, completion of the security guard station in the basement and installation of security and fire protection systems. The front walkway was relaid in red brick and repairs were made to the stone wall and iron fence which date to the mid-1820s and the first executive residence/capitol.

Christopher Bond was re-elected Governor in 1980, and two weeks after leading the Grand March with her husband at his inaugural in January 1981, Mrs. Bond gave birth to their son, Samuel Reid Bond. The Bonds' return provided momentum for the continued restoration of the Mansion. A comprehensive environmental control system was installed and restoration work began on the Great Hall and Grand Stairway. The 1976 McDonnell gift, coupled with structural funds appropriated by the legislature in 1976 and 1977, were augmented by additional private donations and income from fund-raising projects. MMPI sponsored two benefit auctions in 1981 and 1982 and raised more than $80,000 from the sale of auction items donated by individuals and businesses from across the state.

Under the guidance of the restoration architect and the MMPI Fine Arts Committee, design drawings were completed, fabrics and wall treatments selected and period Renaissance Revival furniture carefully acquired. A significant addition for the Great Hall was a 10-piece Renaissance Revival parlor suite which was displayed in the Smithsonian Institution's "1876: A Centennial Exhibition." Additional pieces typical of the period included exceptional inlay side cabinets, inlay and marble-topped tables, a folding chair, and paired figural lamps. A matched pair of twelve-branch brass and crystal Archer & Pancoast chandeliers, c. 1876, were featured in the Great Hall; a nearly identical fixture accents the curve of the Grand Stairway. The patent 1889 Chickering piano was housed beneath the stairway in

Scaffolding soars 37 feet on the Grand Stairway during Great Hall restoration.

Portrait of Alfred Orr by George Caleb Bingham (1853) donated to Missouri Mansion Preservation, Inc. in 1982.

the Nook. A focal point of the Great Hall was the massive overmantel mirror, a reproduction in solid walnut of the mirror that was installed following the fire in 1905 during the Folk administration. The mirror is among an extensive collection of furniture, accessories and art donated by Mansion benefactor Marvin M. Millsap of Springfield. Period wall treatment, a paper adaptation of gold damask, was selected as a background for the portraits of Missouri First Ladies and the restored portrait of Alfred Orr by George Caleb Bingham, donated to MMPI by Orr's granddaughter, the late Mrs. Aleen Orr Mangum of Monroe City. A documented pattern carpet on the Grand Stairway and ceiling stenciling adapted from an 1869 design provided the finishing touches to the Great Hall, which was dedicated October 22, 1982.

Restoration of both the Double Parlor and the Dining Room proceeded in 1983, again coupling funds from the legislature and MMPI. The effort was bolstered by a benefactor gift from the Allen P. and Josephine B. Green Foundation of Mexico, Missouri, for the Double Parlor restoration.

The ceiling stencil for the Double Parlor was adapted from period color studies by M. César Daly and from Edward L. Henry's oil painting dated 1872 of a Brooklyn Heights parlor. The richly painted and stenciled ceiling colors—gray-blues, ivory, rose and burgundy accented with gold leaf—are complemented by elaborate draperies and stenciled panelized wall treatment similar to those found in the 1870 Lockwood-Mathews House in Norwalk, Connecticut. A bordered Wilton carpet in a documented pattern from the 1869 Old Merchant's House in New York City completes the room. Featured in the Double Parlor are a Steinway piano, a fringed circular ottoman and a large Renaissance Revival parlor suite attributed to John Jelliff, one of the finest furniture makers of the mid-nineteenth century. Exquisite marquetry cabinets, tables and pedestals give a period warmth. The overmantel mirror, the official gift of Governor and Mrs. Bond during their second term, was unveiled as part of the Double Parlor dedication ceremony held on August 20, 1983.

A benefactor gift from Mr. and Mrs. R. Crosby Kemper and The Crosby Kemper Foundations of Kansas City for the Dining Room enabled MMPI to complete restoration of the public rooms on the first floor. For the Dining Room, architect Ted Wofford adapted a tripartite period wallpaper based on the design and color concepts described in Christopher Dresser's books in which the great Aesthetic Movement botanist and designer set forth ideal decorations for dining rooms, including even the formulas of key paint colors. The wallpaper design uses the motif of Missouri dogwood and hawthorn blossoms printed in gold and silver on dramatic red and blue ground papers representative of period colors.

In addition to the inlaid border accenting the flooring of each restored room, the Dining Room floor incorporates an inlaid center medallion of walnut and oak, similar to those in other houses by Barnett. The sideboard, acquired during the Edwards administration (1844-1848), remains an integral part of the Dining Room. Of 1820 vintage, the piece is nearly identical to one in Andrew Jackson's home, "The Hermitage," in Nashville, Tennessee, that was purchased in May 1821 by Rachel Jackson from François Seignouret, a prominent French cabinetmaker in New Orleans.

On display in the Dining Room are pieces of the silver service from the *U.S.S. Missouri* returned to the Mansion in 1982 after being on loan to the Harry S. Truman Library and Museum. (One of the 18 place settings, each consisting of 14 pieces, remains on loan to the library.) The 112-pint sterling punch bowl and serving tray date to 1904 and the earlier battleship named *Missouri.* The 281-piece silver set, funded by the legislature, was presented by Governor Donnelly to President Truman in December 1948 for the new *Missouri* which was launched on January 29, 1944. The Japanese surrender ending World War II took place aboard the "Mighty Mo."

In addition to accelerating the pace of restoration, MMPI expanded its educational programs. Public tours of the Mansion, held regularly two days a week, continued during restoration and visitors were able to view the artisans at work. The number of visitors increased dramatically from 30,000 in 1981 to 80,000 the following year.

As an extension of the public tour program, MMPI developed a series of three slide presentations about the Mansion, its restoration and its former residents. A traveling exhibit of materials used in the project is available with the restoration presentation. The

Mansion Ballroom (to be restored) with billiard table, c. 1885.

slide programs are given statewide on request by members of MMPI's Speakers Bureau. The recently updated "People's Mansion" slide program features the newly restored first-floor area as well as views of the private quarters on the second floor and the ballroom and guest bedrooms on the third floor. The ballroom contains a Renaissance Revival piano and the c. 1885 billiard table.

A benefactor grant from the Mary Ranken Jordan and Ettie A. Jordan Charitable Foundation of St. Louis has helped complete the restoration of the first floor and supported MMPI's statewide educational programs. Individual educational programs also have been sponsored by the Missouri Arts Council and The Missouri Committee for the Humanities, Inc.

A major project of MMPI in 1983 was the publication of *PAST & REPAST,* a narrative of the history and hospitality of the Missouri Executive Mansion, made possible through a benefactor gift from the Whitaker Foundation of St. Louis, Urban C. Bergbauer, Trustee.

With the first-floor public rooms completed by the end of 1983, MMPI's future restoration focus will center on the semipublic spaces of the upper floors: the historic Stark bedroom on the second floor at the top of the Grand Stairway and the third-floor ballroom and three guest bedrooms. Exterior restoration will include reconstruction of the cornice on the front portico and the first-floor windows on the south bay of the Mansion.

Traditional entertaining continued during the second Bond administration with legislative dinners and other official func-

Former Prime Minister of Great Britain Edward Heath with the Bonds in the Mansion Library, May 1982.

tions. Dignitaries entertained at the Mansion included former Prime Minister Edward Heath of Great Britain and the Japanese Ambassador to the United States, Yoshio Okawara. An innovative "first" occurred when tea was served one afternoon from the scaffolding in the Great Hall. The Mansion Rose Garden was the scene of a wedding uniting close family friends of the Bonds. Whether a picnic, a gala or a lemonade party on the swing for Sam, the tradition of hospitality, established and maintained by First Families for more than a century is being continued.

In its long and colorful history, Missouri has played a vital role in the development of the nation, and for more than a hundred years the Executive Mansion on the bluff above the Missouri River has witnessed the continuing chronicle of state and human events. First Families from varied backgrounds and Missourians and visitors from near and far have made it a living symbol of the warmth and hospitality of the state.

The Mansion is a precious resource, a repository of aesthetic and historical treasures, connecting us to a life far wider than our own. It commemorates the past and welcomes the generations of the future.

"For, indeed, the greatest glory of a building is not in its stones, or in its gold. Its glory is in its Age, and in that deep sense of voicefulness, of stern watching, of mysterious sympathy, nay, even of approval or condemnation, which we feel in walls that have long been washed by the passing waves of humanity. It is in their lasting witness against men, in their quiet contrast with the transitional character of all things, in the strength which, through the lapse of seasons and times, and the decline and birth of dynasties, and the changing of the face of the earth, and of the limits of the sea, maintains its sculptured shapeliness for a time insuperable, connects forgotten and following ages with each other, and half constitutes the identity, as it concentrates the sympathy, of nations . . . ."

JOHN RUSKIN
The Seven Lamps of Architecture, 1849

FIRST FLOOR

PORCH

KITCHEN

DINING ROOM

NOOK

DOUBLE PARLOR

GREAT HALL

LIBRARY

DOUBLE PARLOR

Current floor plans of Executive Mansion's three levels. Funds raised by Missouri Mansion Preservation, Inc. are used for the restoration of the first-floor public rooms, the second-floor historic Stark Bedroom and the semipublic rooms on the third floor as well as for educational programs. The First Family quarters are located on the second floor. The restoration is a joint project of Missouri Mansion Preservation, Inc. and the State of Missouri.

SECOND FLOOR

PORCH

BEDROOM

MASTER BEDROOM

UPPER HALL

LIVING ROOM

STARK BEDROOM

STUDY

DINING ROOM

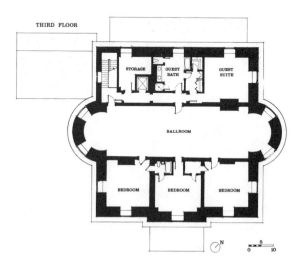

THIRD FLOOR

STORAGE

GUEST BATH

GUEST SUITE

BALLROOM

BEDROOM

BEDROOM

BEDROOM

N

5
0   10

59

*First floor prior to
restoration, 1973.*

Library

Great Hall

*Restored Libra
dedicated August 10, 19*

Restored Great Hall,
dedicated October 22, 1982.

Christmas in the Great
Hall showcasing the
restored overmantel
mirror and the antique
toy collection.

Detail of stenciled Great
Hall ceiling.

*Dining Room, featuring
c.1820 Edwards sideboard
and silver punch bowl
from the U.S.S.
Missouri.*

*First floor prior to
restoration, 1973.*

Double Parlor

Dining Room

HOSPITALITY

Yuletide Dinner

December 15, 1982
Executive Mansion

...

Salmon Mousse

...

Roast Beef Tenderloin
Béarnaise Sauce

...

Pattypan Squash with Puréed Peas
Carrots Cointreau

...

Cranberry Sorbet

...

Bibb Lettuce · Lemon Dressing
Brie

...

Chocolate Amaretto Mousse

...

Café Brûlot

State Dinner
May 26, 1983
Executive Mansion

...

Spring Asparagus Soup
Caraway Wafers
...
Butterflied Leg of Lamb
...
Eggplant & Pepper Gratin
Tabbouleh
...
Lemon Sorbet

...

Romaine Salad · Champagne Dressing
Montrachet
...
Apricot Mousse · Apricot Sauce
...
Demitasse

AT THE BEGINNING

Egg Timbale with Caviar Sauce

⅓	cup sour cream
⅓	cup mayonnaise
	Salt and freshly ground pepper to taste
2	dozen hard-cooked eggs, very coarsely chopped

CAVIAR SAUCE:

1	2-ounce jar red caviar
¾	cup sour cream
¾	cup mayonnaise
	Juice of ½ lemon
½	teaspoon onion juice

Combine sour cream, mayonnaise, salt and pepper. Taste and adjust seasoning. Add just enough of the sour cream mixture to bind the eggs so they are fairly firm and able to hold the shape of the mold. Pack into a well-oiled 6-cup ring mold. Refrigerate until well chilled.

Reserve a small amount of the caviar to garnish timbale. Combine all ingredients, mix well. Refrigerate.

To serve, unmold timbale on a serving platter. Put Caviar Sauce into a small bowl and place in center of mold. Serve with pumpernickel rounds.

20 servings

Every buffet table should include an egg dish and this one is the pièce de résistance.

ecipes with capitalized titles in the First Lady's comments can be found in the index.

Avocado Piquante

The avocado is a gastronomic chameleon. Nut-like in taste, it is a perfect foil for other flavors, with a special affinity for tomato and onion. We selected this simple dish as a first course when the former Prime Minister of Great Britain, Edward Heath, was our guest for dinner on March 1, 1982.

2	tablespoons butter
2	tablespoons ketchup
2	tablespoons cider vinegar
2	tablespoons sugar
2	tablespoons water
1	tablespoon Worcestershire sauce
2	tablespoons prepared chili sauce
2	to 3 avocados, unpeeled, halved and seeded

Place all ingredients, except avocados, in a double boiler. Stir over simmering water until mixture thickens. Remove from heat, cool. Pour sauce into each avocado half and serve as a first course.

4 to 6 servings

Missouri Pâté

4	tablespoons unsalted butter
½	pound fresh mushrooms, chopped
1	shallot, minced
2	tablespoons bourbon
1	tablespoon cognac
8	ounces liverwurst
2	8-ounce packages cream cheese, softened
1	teaspoon chopped fresh dill
1	teaspoon chopped parsley
2	teaspoons Dijon mustard
	Salt and freshly ground pepper to taste

Melt butter in a skillet. Sauté mushrooms and shallot until soft. Stir in bourbon and cognac, cool.

Place mushroom mixture and remaining ingredients in a food processor or blender, process until very smooth. Transfer to a crock or serving bowl. Refrigerate for at least 24 hours before serving. Garnish with sprigs of fresh dill. Serve with party rye and cornichons.

12 servings

A well-spiced pâté is a convenient dish for a country picnic or a festive buffet table. Cornichons add an elegant touch to this mildly flavored regional version of a classic.

Spinach Pâté

An appetizing way to showcase the salmon caviar that Kit brings back from his Alaskan fishing trips. Lovely served on crystal salad plates as a first course.

1¼	pounds fresh spinach, stemmed
	Unsalted butter
3	eggs
¾	cup heavy cream
½	cup white albacore tuna packed in oil, drained and flaked
½	cup minced green onions, including tops
1	tablespoon fresh lemon juice
⅓	cup soft fresh white bread crumbs
1	teaspoon salt
⅛	teaspoon freshly ground pepper
	Salmon caviar
	Lemon wedges

Preheat oven to 375°.

Drop spinach into a 4-quart pan of boiling salted water. Cook 2 to 3 minutes or until barely tender. Rinse under cold water, drain and thoroughly dry. Chop coarsely, set aside.

Combine eggs, cream, tuna, green onions and lemon juice in a food processor or blender, purée. Place tuna mixture, bread crumbs, spinach, salt and pepper in a bowl, mix well, set aside.

Butter bottom of 8½ x 4½-inch loaf pan, line the bottom with wax paper and grease paper lightly with unsalted butter.

Transfer mixture to loaf pan, cover with aluminum foil. Set in a large baking dish and fill baking dish with boiling water half-way up side of loaf pan. Place dish in center of oven and bake 1 hour or until a knife inserted in middle of pâté comes out clean but moist.

Remove pâté from oven, cool on rack to room temperature.

Refrigerate 3 hours or until thoroughly chilled. Unmold on serving platter. Top with a row of salmon caviar down the middle, lengthwise, of the pâté. Arrange enough lemon wedges for each serving on platter, garnish with sprigs of parsley. To serve, cut pâté into ½-inch slices with a long thin-bladed knife. If desired, additional salmon caviar may be served with pâté.

6 to 8 servings

Tuna Pâté

An inspired and inexpensive seafood hors d'oeuvre.

10	ounces canned white albacore tuna, packed in oil, drained*
1	cup butter, softened
2	to 3 drops lemon juice
2	to 3 drops Tabasco sauce
10	medium shrimp, cooked, shelled and minced
3	tablespoons coarsely chopped pimiento
2	tablespoons drained tiny capers
	Salt and freshly ground pepper to taste

Combine tuna, butter, lemon juice and Tabasco in a food processor or blender, process until mixture is smooth. Transfer to a bowl, add shrimp, pimiento and capers, mix well. Season with salt and pepper, taste and adjust seasoning (pâté must be highly seasoned).

Pack into a well-oiled 3-cup loaf pan or mold, chill 24 hours. To serve, let stand 30 minutes at room temperature, unmold on a plate. Garnish with parsley or watercress sprigs and sliced stuffed olives. Serve with buttered toast rounds.

*Do not substitute water-packed tuna

10 servings

Mock Boursin
au Poivre

2	8-ounce packages cream cheese, softened
2	garlic cloves, crushed
2	teaspoons caraway seeds
2	teaspoons dried basil leaves
2	teaspoons dried dill weed
2	tablespoons snipped chives
	Lawry's seasoning salt to taste
2	tablespoons lemon pepper

Place all ingredients, except lemon pepper, in a food processor or blender, process until smooth. Taste and adjust seasoning. Shape into a ball, roll in lemon pepper, refrigerate.

Note: The flavor improves if cheese ball is allowed to stand for 24 hours.

8 to 10 servings

Whether a crystal bowl of Greek olives or a morsel of robust cheddar, the appetizer is firmly entrenched in the American entertaining scene. Try this simple yet elegant version of the "real thing."

Decorated Cheese Wheel

6	8-ounce packages cream cheese, softened
½	cup chopped green onions, including tops
1	garlic clove, minced
8	ounces sharp cheddar cheese, grated
8	ounces Roquefort cheese, softened
2	tablespoons red caviar
2	tablespoons chopped black olives
2	tablespoons minced fresh parsley
2	tablespoons chopped pimiento
2	tablespoons crisply cooked diced bacon
2	tablespoons chopped pitted green olives
2	tablespoons black caviar
2	tablespoons chopped capers

Mix 2 packages of cream cheese with green onions and garlic, set aside. Mix 2 packages of cream cheese with cheddar cheese, set aside. Mix remaining 2 packages of cream cheese with Roquefort cheese, set aside.

Line bottom of a well-oiled 8- to 10-inch round spring-form pan with wax paper, oil paper. Carefully layer cheeses in pan in order mixed, refrigerate. To serve loosen cheese from side of pan with moistened thin-bladed knife, invert on serving dish. Remove wax paper.

Thoroughly drain caviars, olives, pimiento and capers.

Using kitchen twine, mark top of cheese in 8 pie-shaped sections for toppings. Cover each section with 1 of the 8 toppings in order given. The more precise the division between the toppings, the more attractive the appetizer will be. Refrigerate until ready to serve with Melba toast rounds or crackers.

Note: Bleu Cheese may be substituted for Roquefort.

40 servings

Cheddar Cheese and Chutney Spread

2	3-ounce packages cream cheese, softened
4	ounces sharp cheddar cheese, grated
3	tablespoons dry sherry
¾	teaspoon curry powder, or to taste
¼	teaspoon salt
½	cup prepared chutney

Combine all ingredients, except chutney, mix well. Place in an oiled mold or bowl, chill. Before serving, unmold on a plate and pour chutney over the top. Garnish with watercress. Serve with assorted crackers and apple slices.

1½ cups

Great for a Sunday afternoon of televised football. Also a nice choice for a cocktail buffet.

Sweet and Sour
Meat Balls

A handsome silver chafing dish, the official gift of Governor and Mrs. John Dalton, anchors almost every buffet table at the Mansion. By popular request, it frequently holds these savory meat balls.

5	pounds ground chuck
1	pound ground pork
4	eggs
4	teaspoons salt
2	teaspoons pepper
1	teaspoon nutmeg
3	tablespoons Lawry's seasoning salt
4	cups light cream
1	large onion, finely chopped
1	12-ounce box bread crumbs
	Vegetable oil

SWEET AND SOUR SAUCE:

4	13-ounce cans chunk pineapple
½	cup cornstarch
1	cup wine vinegar
2	cups brown sugar
¼	cup soy sauce
1	green pepper, finely diced

Combine all ingredients, except vegetable oil. Shape mixture into balls about 1 inch in diameter, brown in oil. Drain, cool and refrigerate.

Drain pineapple, retaining juice. Add enough water to juice to make 4 cups. Dissolve cornstarch in vinegar. Combine all ingredients, except green pepper. Cook, stirring constantly, until thickened. Add green pepper, heat thoroughly.

To serve, heat meat balls in sauce. Transfer to a chafing dish.

9 dozen

Sombrero Spread

1	pound ground chuck
¼	cup chopped onion
¼	cup extra-hot ketchup
1½	teaspoons chili powder, or to taste
½	teaspoon salt
1	8-ounce can red kidney beans, undrained and mashed
¼	cup drained chopped pimiento-stuffed olives
½	cup chopped onion
½	cup shredded sharp cheddar cheese

Brown meat and onion in a skillet, drain. Stir in ketchup, chili powder, salt and beans. (Spread may now be refrigerated for several days.) Heat thoroughly. Place hot mixture in chafing dish.

On top of meat mixture, arrange a circle of olives at center, encircle olives with a ring of onions and then enclose both with a circle of cheese. Serve hot with tortilla chips.

Note: To aid in washing chafing dish, coat inside with vegetable spray.

12 servings

A tasty offering. For additional flavor, add guacamole and sour cream to the toppings.

Crabmeat Carolyn

Easy and delicious. If available, fresh dill is particularly nice as a garnish.

1	8-ounce package cream cheese, softened
2	tablespoons Worcestershire sauce
1	small onion, grated
1	tablespoon lime juice
3	tablespoons fresh lemon juice, divided
	Garlic salt to taste
2	6-ounce packages frozen Alaskan king crabmeat, defrosted
¾	cup prepared chili sauce

Thoroughly combine cream cheese, Worcestershire sauce, onion, lime juice and 2 tablespoons of lemon juice. Add garlic salt, mix. Taste and adjust seasoning. Mound on a 12-inch platter.

Drain, rinse and refresh frozen crabmeat by tossing with remaining tablespoon of lemon juice.

Pour chili sauce on cream cheese mixture and sprinkle with crabmeat. Garnish with parsley and serve with crackers.

Note: Canned crabmeat may be substituted.

12 to 15 servings

Curry Caper Dip

1	cup mayonnaise
½	cup sour cream
1	teaspoon crushed fines herbes
¼	teaspoon salt
⅛	teaspoon curry, or to taste
1	tablespoon grated onion
1	tablespoon chopped fresh parsley
1½	teaspoons lemon juice
2	teaspoons drained capers
½	teaspoon Worcestershire sauce

Mix all ingredients, chill. Serve with crudités. For a colorful presentation, spoon the dip into a hollowed-out red cabbage or eggplant.

1½ cups

Cocktail buffets at the Mansion frequently feature this dip with huge trays of crudités. Careful blanching of raw vegetables such as broccoli, carrots, asparagus, green beans and Brussels sprouts greatly enhances both the appearance and the flavor. Time consuming, but worth it.

Green Herb Sauce

Truly versatile. The fresh and vibrant color of this sauce makes it the ideal accompaniment for cold smoked trout or Poached Salmon on the Grill.

½	bunch watercress, stemmed and coarsely chopped
½	bunch scallions, chopped
6	ounces fresh spinach, stemmed and coarsely chopped
¼	cup chopped fresh dill
2	cups mayonnaise
¼	cup sour cream
¼	cup fresh lemon juice
2	tablespoons finely grated onion
	Dash Worcestershire sauce
	Salt and freshly ground pepper to taste

In a food processor or blender, place watercress, scallions, spinach and dill, chop until fine and transfer to a bowl. Combine remaining ingredients in machine, mix well. Taste and adjust seasoning. Fold into chopped greens, refrigerate overnight. Serve as a dipping sauce with seafood, chicken or crudités.

3½ cups

Caraway Wafers

1	cup flour
½	cup unsalted butter, softened
1	5-ounce jar Old English Cheese spread
1	tablespoon caraway seeds
	Salt to taste
	Cayenne pepper to taste

Combine flour, butter and cheese in a food processor or blender, process well. Add caraway seeds, salt and cayenne, mix well. Taste and adjust seasoning. Shape into a 1½-inch-in-diameter roll. Wrap in wax paper, refrigerate until well chilled.

Preheat oven to 375°.

Cut into thin slices, bake on ungreased cookie sheets for 8 minutes or until lightly browned. Cool on racks.

6 to 7 dozen

Crispy and tasty!

Texas Cheese Wafers

1	cup butter, softened
2	cups flour
8	ounces cheddar cheese, grated
½	teaspoon cayenne pepper, or to taste
½	teaspoon salt
2	cups toasted rice cereal

Preheat oven to 350°.

Cut butter into flour. Add cheese and seasonings, mix lightly. Fold in cereal. By teaspoons, roll into balls and place on ungreased cookie sheets. Dip fork tines in flour and press tines into each wafer in a crisscross pattern.

Bake 12 to 15 minutes or until lightly browned. Cool on racks. Store airtight.

Note: For a hotter version, increase cayenne to 1 teaspoon.

5 dozen

During the 1974 Southern Governors' Conference, Lady Bird Johnson entertained the First Ladies for tea at the Johnson Library. These peppery wafers were a standout, and Mrs. Johnson kindly supplied us with the recipe.

Seasoned Nuts

Zesty tidbits for munching or for giving to friends and neighbors during the holidays.

HERB PEPPER ALMONDS:

4	tablespoons butter
2	cups whole almonds
4	teaspoons herb pepper seasoning
	Kosher salt to taste

DEVILED PECANS:

4	tablespoons butter
¼	cup Worcestershire sauce
10	dashes Tabasco sauce
4	cups pecan halves
3	tablespoons garlic salt

MEXICAN WALNUTS:

4	tablespoons butter
4	cups walnut halves
1	tablespoon chili powder
2	teaspoons cumin seeds

Preheat oven to 325°.

Each recipe: Melt butter in a jelly roll pan. Stir in nuts and seasonings. Bake 20 minutes, stirring occasionally. Remove from pan with slotted spoon, drain on paper towels.

2 to 4 cups

White Sangria

1	bottle dry white wine, chilled
½	cup Cointreau
¼	cup sugar
	Ice cubes
1	10-ounce bottle of club soda, chilled
1	orange, sliced
1	lemon, sliced
2	limes, cut into wedges

Combine wine, Cointreau and sugar in a glass pitcher, mix well. Stir in ice, club soda and fruit when ready to serve. Garnish with mint sprigs.

1½ quarts

Preface a summer patio supper with this delightful concoction and Seasoned Nuts or Mock Boursin au Poivre.

Strawberry Wine Slush

1	6-ounce can frozen limeade concentrate
1⅓	cups sauterne
16	ice cubes, crushed
1	pint fresh strawberries

About 15 minutes before serving, or up to a week ahead, combine ingredients in a food processor or blender, purée. Serve immediately or pour into a container and freeze. To serve, pour into chilled glasses and garnish with lime slices. If frozen, defrost and stir well before serving.

5 generous servings

Titillate your palate with this summer cooler before a lunch of Chicken Pasta Primavera.

Hot Cranberry Punch

⅓	cup packed brown sugar
½	cup water
½	teaspoon ground cloves
¼	teaspoon allspice
¼	teaspoon cinnamon
½	teaspoon nutmeg
	Pinch of salt
1	quart cranberry juice cocktail
2	cups unsweetened pineapple juice
	Confectioners' sugar to taste
	Butter

Combine brown sugar, water, spices and salt. Bring to a boil, add juices and confectioners' sugar according to desired sweetness, heat to second boil. Serve hot with pats of butter floating in cups.

8 servings

Hot Mulled Wine

2	cups water
4	cups sugar
4	sticks cinnamon
1	teaspoon whole cloves
3	medium oranges, thinly sliced
1	lemon, thinly sliced
1	gallon dry red wine, room temperature

Combine all ingredients, except wine, in an 8-quart saucepan. Bring to a boil, continue boiling for 5 minutes, stirring occasionally.

Reduce heat to medium, pour in wine. Heat, stirring occasionally, until piping hot, but do not boil. Use strainer or slotted spoon to remove spices and fruit. Ladle into cups or mugs and garnish each serving with a cinnamon stick and a dash of nutmeg.

18 servings

An invigorating libation following an afternoon of ice skating or cross country skiing.

FROM THE BREAD BASKET

Blueberry Coffee Cake

2¼	cups flour, sifted, divided
1	tablespoon baking powder
½	cup plus 2 tablespoons sugar
½	teaspoon salt
1	egg
¼	cup vegetable oil
1	cup milk
¾	cup chopped English walnuts
1¼	cups fresh blueberries
2	tablespoons butter, softened
3	tablespoons brown sugar
⅛	teaspoon cinnamon

Preheat oven to 375°.

Combine 2 cups of flour and the baking powder in a food processor or blender, mix. Add sugar, salt, egg, oil and milk. Mix, using a quick on-and-off technique, until flour is incorporated. Lightly blend in nuts and blueberries.

Turn mixture into a well-greased and floured 9-inch square pan.

Place butter, brown sugar, cinnamon and remaining flour in a food processor or blender, mix until crumbly. Sprinkle over coffee cake.

Bake 1 hour and 10 minutes or until a toothpick inserted in the center comes out clean. Serve warm or cool on rack.

Note: Frozen unsweetened blueberries may be substituted.

8 servings

Always a good choice for a coffee, this is excellent as a dessert served with Crème Fraîche or a scoop of vanilla ice cream.

Gooey Butter
Coffee Cake

1	16-ounce box pound cake mix
4	eggs, divided
½	cup butter, melted
1	16-ounce box confectioners' sugar
1	8-ounce package cream cheese, softened
1½	tablespoons vanilla extract

Preheat oven to 300°.

Combine cake mix, 2 eggs and the butter. Pour into a well-greased 8 x 12-inch baking pan. Reserve 2 tablespoons of sugar. Combine cream cheese, vanilla, remaining eggs and sugar, mix well. Spread over batter.

Bake 15 minutes. Remove from oven, sprinkle reserved sugar on top. Return to oven, continue to bake for 25 minutes. Serve warm or cool on rack.

10 to 12 servings

Carrot Bread

2	cups sifted flour
½	teaspoon salt
2	teaspoons baking soda
2	teaspoons cinnamon
¼	cup chopped nuts
1	cup vegetable oil
1	teaspoon vanilla extract
1½	cups sugar
3	eggs, beaten
2	cups grated carrots
1	cup raisins or ½ cup raisins and ½ cup coconut (optional)

Preheat oven to 350°.

Combine flour, salt, soda and cinnamon, sift into a large mixing bowl. Add remaining ingredients, mix well.

Turn into a well-greased 9 x 5-inch loaf pan. Let stand 20 minutes before baking 1 hour or until done. Remove from pan, cool on rack.

1 loaf

An easy way to get children to eat carrots.

Cherry Pecan Bread

Serve piping hot from the oven with a cup of freshly brewed coffee and the morning paper and surprise someone you love with breakfast in bed.

¾	cup sugar
½	cup butter, softened
2	eggs
2	cups sifted flour
1	teaspoon baking soda
½	teaspoon salt
1	cup buttermilk
1	cup chopped pecans
1	10-ounce jar maraschino cherries, drained and chopped
1	teaspoon vanilla extract

Preheat oven to 350°.

Cream sugar, butter and eggs until light and fluffy. In a separate bowl, sift together flour, baking soda and salt, stir into creamed mixture. Add buttermilk, mix well. Stir in nuts, cherries and vanilla.

Turn batter into a well-greased 9 x 5-inch loaf pan. Bake 55 to 60 minutes. Remove from pan, cool on rack.

1 loaf

Poppy Seed Bread

3	cups flour, sifted
1½	teaspoons salt
1½	teaspoons baking powder
3	eggs, lightly beaten
1½	cups milk
2¼	cups sugar
1	cup plus 2 tablespoons vegetable oil
1½	teaspoons vanilla extract
1½	teaspoons almond flavoring
1½	teaspoons butter flavoring
1½	tablespoons poppy seeds

GLAZE:

½	teaspoon butter flavoring
½	teaspoon almond flavoring
½	teaspoon vanilla extract
¼	cup orange juice
¾	cup sugar

Preheat oven to 350°.

Combine flour, salt and baking powder in a large mixing bowl. Mix together eggs, milk, sugar, oil, vanilla and flavorings. Add to dry ingredients, mix well. Fold in poppy seeds.

Turn into 2 well-greased 9 x 5-inch loaf pans and bake 1 hour or until done.

Mix all ingredients.

Remove bread from pans. Brush on glaze while loaves are still hot, cool on rack.

2 loaves

Offer this with your favorite chicken salad served in a papaya half or melon ring for lunch or with other breads for a brunch.

Mexican Corn Bread

¡Olé!
For an ethnic
medley, serve with
Hungarian Cabbage
Soup.

2	eggs
¼	cup vegetable oil
1	to 4 canned green chilies, chopped (to taste)
1	8½-ounce can creamed corn
½	cup sour cream
1	cup yellow cornmeal
½	teaspoon salt
2	teaspoons baking powder
2	cups shredded sharp cheddar cheese, divided

Preheat oven to 350°.

Beat eggs and oil. Stir in green chilies, corn, sour cream, cornmeal, salt, baking powder and 1½ cups of cheese, mix well.

Pour into a well-greased 9-inch baking pan. Sprinkle remaining cheese over top, bake 1 hour. Best served hot.

8 servings

Party Pinwheels

1	8-ounce package crescent rolls, from the dairy case
2	teaspoons sesame seeds
½	teaspoon caraway seeds
1	teaspoon poppy seeds
2	tablespoons unsalted butter, melted

Preheat oven to 375°.

Separate crescent rolls into four rectangles on a pastry board. Eliminate the diagonal cut on each rectangle by moistening and pressing together the serrated edges.

Mix all seeds together. With basting brush, spread butter on dough, sprinkle seeds evenly over butter. Roll like a jelly roll, moisten seam and seal tightly.

Spray a freezer-safe dish with vegetable spray. Place rolls on dish, freeze until firm enough to slice.

Spray cookie sheet with vegetable spray. Cut rolls into ½-inch slices. Bake 5 minutes or until lightly browned. Serve immediately or at room temperature.

3 dozen

You don't have to be a bread maker to prepare this welcome alternative to French bread or dinner rolls.

FROM THE TUREEN

Avocado Senegalese Soup

1	medium onion, chopped
1	rib celery, minced
2	tablespoons butter
1	tablespoon flour
2	teaspooons curry powder, or to taste
1	tart green apple, peeled, cored and chopped
4	cups chicken broth, divided
1	avocado, peeled, seeded and chopped
1	cup light cream
	Salt to taste

Sauté onion and celery in butter until limp and translucent. Add flour and curry powder, stirring constantly until thoroughly blended. Stir in apple and 2 cups of broth, cook over low heat until apples are soft.

Transfer mixture to a food processor or blender, add avocado, process until smooth. Combine with remaining broth and cream, add salt, stir thoroughly. Taste and adjust seasoning, chill. Serve garnished with thin slices of avocado and a dusting of coconut that has been lightly toasted in the oven.

6 servings

Very delicate and elusive in flavor.

Cold Borscht with Cucumber

Cucumber is the magic ingredient in this classic cold soup. Store the soup bowls in the freezer until serving time for added appeal.

2	small bunches of fresh beets, scraped and diced
6	cups beef stock
2	teaspoons sugar, or to taste
1	tablespoon lemon juice
1	cucumber, peeled, seeded and diced
	Salt to taste
½	cup sour cream

Combine beets with stock, bring to a boil, cover. Simmer 40 minutes, strain, reserve liquid, discard beets. Add sugar and lemon juice, mix well, chill. Add cucumber and salt. Taste and adjust seasoning. To serve, top with a spoonful of sour cream and garnish with sprigs of fresh dill.

6 to 8 servings

Chilled Corn Chowder

A refreshing start for a poolside supper of charcoaled steaks, sautéed zucchini and sliced tomatoes.

1⅓	cups corn, cooked and cut from the cob
⅓	cup green onion tops, cut into ¼-inch pieces
1	quart buttermilk
	Juice of ½ lime
	Salt and freshly ground white pepper to taste
3	to 4 sprigs of fresh dill

Combine cooled corn and green onion tops with buttermilk. Add lime juice, season with salt and pepper, chill. Taste and adjust seasoning. Garnish with sprigs of fresh dill.

4 to 6 servings

Cold Cucumber Soup

3	cucumbers, peeled, seeded and sliced
2	tablespoons butter
3	tablespoons flour
3	cups chicken stock
1	cup milk
	Several slices of onion
½	cup heavy cream
	Salt and freshly ground pepper
	Few drops of green food coloring (optional)

Sauté cucumbers in butter for 10 minutes. Stir in flour and gradually add stock, stirring constantly. Scald milk with onion slices and strain, reserve milk, discard onions. Add milk to stock mixture, simmer slowly 10 minutes. Remove cucumbers from stock mixture and reserve, set mixture aside.

Place cucumbers and 1 cup of stock mixture in a food processor or blender, purée. Combine purée with remaining stock mixture, add cream and season with salt and pepper. (Thoroughly blend in green food coloring.) Chill. Taste and adjust seasoning. Garnish with fresh dill, chives, tarragon or parsley.

Note: Sour cream may be substituted for heavy cream, but should be added after soup is chilled to prevent curdling.

4 to 6 servings

One of the most popular cold soups served at the Mansion. We often ladle it from a large silver punch bowl in the Great Hall before guests are seated for lunch in the Dining Room.

Frosted Tomato Bisque

We pack a thermos of this for sandbar picnics at the Lake of the Ozarks and serve it in plastic glasses. For an elegant first course, present in crystal bowls.

1	14½-ounce can Italian plum tomatoes
1	10½-ounce can beef consommé
½	cup dry sherry
1	or 2 teaspoons finely chopped onion (to taste)
½	teaspoon celery salt
½	teaspoon parsley flakes
½	teaspoon curry powder, or to taste
½	to 1 teaspoon salt (to taste)
½	teaspoon freshly ground pepper
1½	cups sour cream

Drain tomatoes, reserve liquid. Seed tomatoes.

Place all ingredients in a food processor or blender, process thoroughly, chill. Taste and adjust seasoning. Garnish with a spoonful of additional sour cream and seasoned croutons.

Note: This soup may be made a day ahead.

4 to 6 servings

Strawberry Soup

2	cups fresh strawberries
2	cups unsweetened pineapple juice
⅓	cup confectioners' sugar, sifted
½	cup Burgundy or other dry red wine
½	cup sour cream

Place strawberries in a food processor or blender, purée. Add pineapple juice and sugar, process until smooth. Add Burgundy and sour cream, mix well, chill. Garnish with whipped cream, sliced strawberries and mint leaves.

4 to 6 servings

Cold fruit soups are an unexpected but welcome prelude to a light luncheon featuring seafood or chicken salad.

Missouri Apple Soup

Cultivated since ancient times, the apple is the symbol of earthly joy and laughter. This flavorful soup is guaranteed to produce smiles.

2	tablespoons butter
2	medium onions, thinly sliced
6	red Jonathan apples, peeled, cored and diced
4	cups chicken broth
2	tablespoons sugar
1	tablespoon curry powder, or to taste
	Salt and freshly ground white pepper to taste
1	to 2 cups light cream (to taste)

In a Dutch oven, melt butter, sauté onions until transparent. Add apples, broth, sugar and curry powder. Season with salt and pepper. Cook covered over low heat until apples are soft.

Strain apples and onions from broth and reserve, set broth aside. Place apples and onions in a food processor or blender, purée. Add broth, blend well. Add cream according to desired richness, chill. Taste and adjust seasoning. Garnish with thin apple wedges and a sprinkling of sliced almonds.

10 to 12 servings

Pimiento Soup

2	7-ounce cans whole pimientos, drained
1	14½-ounce can whole tomatoes, undrained
	Juice of 1 lemon
1	teaspoon Worchestershire sauce
3	dashes Tabasco sauce
1	14½-ounce can chicken broth
½	cup heavy cream
	Salt and freshly ground pepper to taste

Rinse pimientos to remove seeds. Drain tomatoes, reserve liquid. Press tomatoes through a sieve to remove seeds and pulp. Combine pimientos, tomatoes and reserved liquid, lemon juice, Worcestershire and Tabasco in a food processor or blender. Process on high speed 15 seconds or until the vegetables are puréed. With motor running, add broth and cream. Season with salt and pepper, chill. Taste and adjust seasoning. Serve topped with a thin slice of lemon and a sprig of parsley.

To serve hot, omit adding cream in food processor or blender. Instead, process purée and broth only, heat. Remove from heat, stir in cream, season with salt and pepper. Garnish with chopped scallions and croutons.

6 servings

After the accolades, tell your guests the name of this surprisingly delicious soup. Equally good served cold or hot.

Curried Pea Soup

Follow this flavorful soup, served hot, with our Tailgate Hero Sandwich and then cheer the Mizzou Tigers on to victory!

1	10-ounce package frozen peas
1	medium onion, sliced
1	small carrot, sliced
1	rib celery with leaves, sliced
1	medium potato, sliced
1	garlic clove, crushed
1	teaspoon salt
1	teaspoon curry powder, or to taste
2	cups chicken stock, divided
1	cup heavy cream

Place vegetables, seasonings and 1 cup of stock in a saucepan, bring to a boil. Cover, reduce heat and simmer 20 to 30 minutes until vegetables are very tender.

Transfer vegetables to a food processor or blender, purée. With the motor running, pour in remaining stock and the cream, chill. Garnish each portion with whipped cream and a mint leaf.

To serve hot, omit adding cream in food processor or blender. Instead, process purée and stock only, heat. Remove from heat, stir in cream. Garnish with a teaspoon of sour cream and crisply cooked crumbled bacon.

4 to 6 servings

Spring Asparagus Soup

1	pound fresh asparagus
5	cups chicken stock
4	tablespoons butter
4	tablespoons flour
1	teaspoon curry powder, or to taste
¾	cup heavy cream
	Salt and freshly ground white pepper to taste
3	egg yolks
	Dash of lemon juice

Remove tough ends from asparagus stalks. Peel stalks, cut off tips and reserve. Cut stalks into 1-inch pieces, combine with stock in a large saucepan. Bring to a boil, reduce heat, cover and simmer for 45 minutes.

While soup is simmering, drop asparagus tips into boiling salted water. Cook 3 minutes or until tender, drain and reserve tips.

Remove stalks from stock. Transfer to a food processor or blender, purée. Add stock, process thoroughly.

Melt butter, add flour and cook 2 minutes without letting it brown. Add puréed stock, stirring, and bring to a boil. Cook, stirring, over low heat until soup thickens and coats the spoon.

Mix curry powder with a little cream, add to soup with asparagus tips. Season with salt and pepper, stir.

Just before serving, combine remaining cream and the egg yolks, add to soup with lemon juice. Taste and adjust seasoning. Reheat, but do not boil. Serve very hot.

4 to 6 servings

The marriage of curry and fresh asparagus is subtle and delicious. I often serve this as the first course of a spring dinner featuring lamb chops or Butterflied Leg of Lamb. Garnish the soup with a grating of orange zest.

Summer Basil Soup

1	cup packed fresh basil leaves*
2	large garlic cloves, minced
1	tablespoon pine nuts
¼	cup grated Parmesan cheese
¼	cup vegetable oil
8	cups chicken stock
¼	cup uncooked spaghetti rings (anellini)
	Salt and freshly ground pepper to taste
2	small zucchini, cut into ¼-inch slices

Place basil, garlic, pine nuts and cheese in a food processor or blender, process until smooth. With the motor running, add oil in a thin stream until thoroughly incorporated, forming a thick paste.

Heat stock in a 4-quart saucepan. Add spaghetti rings, cover, cook 10 minutes. Whisk in basil paste, season with salt and pepper. Add zucchini 2 minutes before serving so it will remain crisp. Taste and adjust seasoning. Serve immediately.

*Only fresh basil does justice to the soup. Do not substitute dried.

8 servings

Hot Clam Soup

16	ounces Clamato juice
1	10½-ounce can beef consommé
1	10¾-ounce can tomato soup
½	soup can of water
1½	teaspoons curry powder, or to taste
1	tablespoon Worcestershire sauce
2	teaspoons soy sauce
½	teaspoon Lawry's seasoned salt
½	teaspoon onion salt
2	tablespoons minced onion
1	lemon wedge
3	tablespoons butter
1	6½-ounce can minced clams, undrained
10	tablespoons dry sherry, divided

Combine all ingredients, except clams and sherry, heat 10 minutes. Remove lemon wedge, discard. Add clams with juice and 2 tablespoons sherry, simmer 1 hour.

To serve, put 1 tablespoon sherry in each serving bowl, add hot soup. Garnish with a dollop of sour cream and sprinkle with dill weed.

8 servings

Serve this spicy soup as a first course of a cozy supper on a wintry night or for a light luncheon followed by salad and dessert.

Hungarian Cabbage Soup

Ladle into sizable soup bowls and savor the unique blend of flavors in front of a crackling fire.

1	cup chopped onion
3	carrots, pared and coarsely chopped
1	bay leaf
2	garlic cloves, chopped
4	pounds beef short ribs
1	teaspoon dried thyme
½	teaspoon paprika
8	cups water
2	16-ounce cans tomatoes
2	teaspoons salt
½	to ¾ teaspoon Tabasco sauce (to taste)
¼	cup chopped parsley
3	tablespoons lemon juice
3	tablespoons sugar
1	16-ounce can sauerkraut
8	cups coarsely shredded cabbage

Preheat oven to 450°.

Place onion, carrots, bay leaf and garlic in a roasting pan, top with short ribs and sprinkle with thyme and paprika. Roast uncovered 20 minutes or until meat is browned.

Transfer to a large kettle, add water, tomatoes, salt and Tabasco. Bring to a boil, cover, simmer 1½ hours. Skim off fat. Add parsley, lemon juice, sugar and sauerkraut. Simmer uncovered 1 hour.

Remove bay leaf, discard. Remove short ribs, discard bones, cut meat into cubes and return to kettle. Add shredded cabbage, cook 8 minutes or until barely done. To serve, garnish with a spoonful of sour cream.

Note: This soup is best made a day or two ahead and reheated before serving.

8 to 10 servings

Sausage Zucchini Soup

1¼	pounds mild Italian sausage (if link sausage, remove casings)
1½	cups sliced celery
4	pounds fresh tomatoes, peeled and cut in wedges
1½	cups tomato juice
1	teaspoon salt
1½	teaspoons Italian seasoning
1	teaspoon sugar
¼	teaspoon garlic salt
2	green peppers, cut into 1-inch pieces
1½	pounds zucchini, cut into ¼-inch slices
1	cup shredded mozzarella cheese

Crumble sausage into a 4-quart saucepan, brown, drain off fat. Add celery, cook 10 minutes. Add tomatoes, juice and seasonings, simmer 10 minutes.

Stir in green peppers, cook 5 minutes. Add zucchini, cook 1 to 2 minutes until barely heated. Caution: Do not overcook zucchini. Sprinkle mozzarella cheese over the top, serve immediately.

Note: If more liquid is desired, add more tomato juice. Two 28-ounce cans Italian plum tomatoes may be substituted for fresh tomatoes.

8 to 10 servings

A hearty soup that is perfect for a late summer or early fall Sunday night supper. It is also an excellent way to use an abundant supply of zucchini and tomatoes from your garden. Serve with crusty French bread and sweet butter.

FROM THE SALAD BOWL

Antipasto Salad

1½	cups vegetable oil
½	cup tarragon vinegar
½	cup chopped fresh parsley
2	teaspoons dried chervil
4	garlic cloves, finely minced
	Salt and freshly ground pepper to taste
1	14-ounce can artichoke hearts, halved
1	6-ounce can pitted black olives
1	8-ounce can hearts of palm, cut into ¾-inch slices
1	8-ounce jar mild pepperoncini
1	pint cherry tomatoes
1	pound fresh mushrooms
1	pound carrots, peeled and cut into ½-inch slices
1	pound celery, cut into 1-inch slices
6	small zucchini, halved and cut into 1-inch slices

Prepare two days before serving.

To make marinade, combine first 5 ingredients in a plastic container large enough to hold all the vegetables. Season with salt and pepper. Drain canned vegetables well.

In boiling salted water, blanch vegetables as follows: mushrooms for 1 minute, carrots for 4 minutes or until tender-crisp, celery for 4 minutes and zucchini for 1 minute. After blanching each vegetable, immediately plunge into a pan of ice water. Drain and pat dry.

Halve tomatoes and drain on paper towels.

Add all vegetables to marinade, toss to coat. Refrigerate 48 hours, stirring occasionally. Taste and adjust seasoning.

To serve, remove from refrigerator and allow vegetables to reach room temperature. Drain in a colander, serve garnished with fresh Italian parsley.

20 servings

A vegetarian's delight and a great make-ahead dish for an alfresco supper.

Tomato and Mozzarella Salad

Serve this as a first course and eliminate a more traditional salad from your dinner menu. As palatable as it is colorful.

2	tablespoons minced fresh basil
1	tablespoon minced fresh parsley
1	large garlic clove, minced
5	tablespoons salad oil
1½	tablespoons red wine vinegar
	Pinch of salt
	Freshly ground pepper to taste
4	large ripe tomatoes, cut into ¼-inch slices
2	8-ounce packages mozzarella, thinly sliced
1	red onion, peeled and sliced into rings
1	can flat anchovy fillets, well drained

Combine basil, parsley, garlic, oil, vinegar and salt in a food processor or blender, process until smooth. Season with pepper, mix, set aside.

On a large platter, alternate and overlap tomato and mozzarella slices. Drizzle dressing over salad. Top with onion rings, pepper to taste and anchovy fillets. Garnish with parsley sprigs and black olives. Serve lightly chilled, but not cold.

4 to 6 servings

Marinated Cherry Tomatoes

2	pints ripe cherry tomatoes
1	teaspoon Dijon mustard
¾	teaspoon sugar
	Salt and freshly ground pepper to taste
¼	cup raspberry vinegar
½	cup peanut oil
¼	cup thinly sliced green onions
1	tablespoon chopped fresh parsley
1	to 2 teaspoons chopped fresh basil (to taste)
3	medium Belgian endives
¼	cup chopped pitted black olives

Halve tomatoes and drain cut side down. Combine mustard, sugar, salt, pepper and vinegar in a food processor or blender. With machine running, add oil in a thin stream until thoroughly incorporated. Taste dressing, adjust seasoning.

In a separate bowl, place tomatoes, green onions, parsley and basil. Toss with 5 tablespoons of dressing, set remainder aside.

To serve, place tomatoes in a glass bowl in the center of a large platter. Cut stem ends off endives, arrange spears in a sunburst design radiating from the tomatoes. Drizzle remaining dressing over endive. Sprinkle with black olives and serve at room temperature.

Note: Tomatoes may be tossed and refrigerated several hours in advance. Allow to return to room temperature before serving.

8 servings

Off-season tomatoes are generally uninspiring and tasteless. By comparison, the small cherry tomatoes which are available even during the winter months have a surprising depth of flavor. They make a colorful addition to any salad.

Asparagus Vinaigrette

Spring is the season of anticipation, and everyone looks forward to the first tender spears of asparagus. This marinated version is a Mansion favorite for large buffets.

2½	pounds fresh asparagus*, peeled and trimmed
¾	cup vegetable oil
¼	cup wine vinegar
2	tablespoons capers
2	teaspoons finely chopped onion
½	teaspoon dried chervil
½	teaspoon dried tarragon
1	teaspoon chopped chives
	Salt and freshly ground pepper to taste

Cook asparagus until barely tender, drain. Place in a covered glass container, set aside.

Combine remaining ingredients, season with salt and pepper, mix well. Pour over asparagus. Cover and refrigerate 24 hours, turning occasionally. Taste and adjust seasoning. To serve, drain asparagus and garnish with additional capers.

Note: Two 10-ounce packages frozen asparagus may be substituted. Defrost and drain, but do not cook.

*Do not use canned asparagus.

8 servings

Italian Green Beans

2	pounds fresh green beans
1	small onion, finely minced
1	small garlic clove, finely minced
½	cup grated fresh Parmesan cheese
6	tablespoons salad oil
2	tablespoons wine vinegar
1	teaspoon Dijon mustard
1	teaspoon salt
¼	teaspoon pepper

Trim ends from green beans and leave whole. Cook in boiling salted water until tender-crisp, drain and cool. Combine green beans with onion and garlic, sprinkle with cheese, set aside.

In another bowl, combine oil, vinegar, mustard, salt and pepper. Pour over bean mixture, toss. To serve, arrange salad on lettuce and garnish with tomato wedges, black olives and anchovy fillets.

Note: Flavor is better if made the day before serving.

8 servings

The perfect summer addition to an antipasto platter or a seasonal substitute for tossed green salad.

Summer Rice Salad

The flavors are enhanced if this colorful salad is refrigerated and then allowed to return to room temperature before serving. Excellent with grilled chicken, lamb or hamburgers.

3	cups steamed rice, cooled to room temperature
¼	cup mayonnaise
½	cup thinly sliced radishes
½	cup thinly sliced scallions
1	sweet red pepper, minced
1	green pepper, minced
2	tablespoons minced sweet gherkins
1	tablespoon minced fresh parsley
1	tablespoon snipped fresh dill
1	tablespoon snipped fresh chives
½	cup fresh lemon juice
2	teaspoons salt
2	garlic cloves, crushed
1¼	cups salad oil
	Salt and freshly ground pepper to taste

Combine first 10 ingredients, mix well, set aside.

Place lemon juice, salt and garlic in a food processor or blender, mix well. With machine running, add oil in a thin stream until thoroughly incorporated. If added too fast, dressing may separate.

Add dressing to rice mixture, season with salt and pepper. Taste and adjust seasoning. To serve, mound on a lettuce leaf and garnish with black olives.

8 to 10 servings

Tabbouleh

2	cups bulgur
2	cucumbers, peeled, seeded and diced
1	tablespoon salt
3	ripe medium tomatoes, peeled, seeded and diced
2	cups finely chopped Italian parsley
2	tablespoons chopped fresh mint, or to taste
1	cup finely chopped scallions
6	tablespoons vegetable oil
5	to 10 tablespoons lemon juice (to taste)
	Salt and freshly ground pepper to taste

Cover bulgur with water, soak 30 minutes in a large bowl (it will quadruple in volume). Squeeze soaked bulgur by hand to eliminate as much water as possible, spread on a dish towel and dry near a sunny window.

Place cucumbers in a colander, add salt and cover with a weighted dish to help release liquid. After 30 minutes, rinse under cold water, drain well, dry on paper towels. In a large serving bowl, mix bulgur, cucumbers, tomatoes, parsley, mint and scallions, set aside.

Combine oil and lemon juice, mix well, season with salt and pepper. Pour dressing over bulgur, toss well. Taste and adjust seasoning. Serve at room temperature. Garnish with lemon slices and chopped parsley.

8 to 10 servings

Familiar flavors combine with the bulgur for an intriguing dish. I find it particularly nice with Lamb Shanks with Chutney or Butterflied Leg of Lamb.

Spinach Salad with Chutney Dressing

An Oriental variation on a familiar theme—spinach, bacon and mushrooms. Delicious and substantial enough for a luncheon entrée.

¾	pound fresh spinach, stemmed and torn
6	mushrooms, sliced
1	cup sliced water chestnuts
6	slices bacon, crisply cooked, drained and crumbled
½	cup shredded Gruyere cheese
¼	cup thinly sliced red onion
¾	cup fresh bean sprouts, drained and patted dry

CHUTNEY DRESSING:

¼	cup wine vinegar
1	garlic clove, crushed
1	tablespoon Dijon mustard
2	teaspoons sugar
⅓	to ½ cup salad oil (to taste)
5	tablespoons prepared chutney
	Salt and freshly ground pepper to taste

Toss spinach with other ingredients, except bean sprouts, set aside.

Note: Salad ingredients may be prepared the day before serving. Package in plastic bags, wrapping spinach in paper towels before packaging. Refrigerate.

Combine vinegar, garlic, mustard and sugar in a food processor or blender mix until smooth. With machine running, pour oil in a thin stream until thoroughly incorporated. Using an on and-off technique, lightly mix in chutney, season with salt and pepper. Taste and adjust seasoning. Refrigerate.

To serve, add bean sprouts to salad greens and toss again with dressing.

8 to 10 servings

Lemon Dressing

7	tablespoons salad oil
2½	tablespoons wine vinegar
⅛	teaspoon nutmeg
½	teaspoon grated lemon rind
½	teaspoon crushed dried tarragon
½	teaspoon salt
	Freshly ground pepper

Combine all ingredients, mix well. Cover and let stand at room temperature for at least 30 minutes, preferably overnight. Refrigerate until ready to use. Toss with mixed greens, mushrooms and chopped parsley. Garnish with toasted pine nuts.

⅔ cup

A frequent choice for Mansion entertaining. Toasted pine nuts somehow heighten the unique and subtle blend of flavors in this dressing.

Champagne Dressing

3	egg yolks
1	tablespoon Dijon mustard
⅓	cup white wine vinegar
¼	cup champagne
	Salt and freshly ground pepper to taste
2	cups corn oil

Combine egg yolks, mustard, vinegar and champagne in a food processor or blender, process 1 minute. Season with salt and pepper. With machine running, add oil in a thin stream until thoroughly incorporated. If added too fast, sauce may separate. Scrape down sides of container, taste and adjust seasoning. Refrigerate until ready to use.

3 cups

A tart but tasty dressing. At the moment of serving, mix into a salad of watercress, romaine or Belgian endive and mushrooms. Also good as a sauce for artichokes and as a dip for crudités.

Tarragon Dressing

Try this savory dressing over a salad of watercress and thinly sliced fresh mushrooms or romaine and curly endive.

1	egg
2	teaspoons dried tarragon
½	bunch parsley, stemmed and chopped
½	teaspoon dry mustard
½	teaspoon salt
¼	teaspoon freshly ground pepper
	Juice of ½ lemon
2	teaspoons chopped shallots
⅔	cup tarragon vinegar
¼	cup minced fresh garlic
3	cups salad oil

Combine all ingredients, except salad oil, in a food processor or blender, mix well. With machine running, add oil in a thin stream until thoroughly incorporated. If added too fast, sauce may separate. Refrigerate until ready to use.

4 cups

Poppy Seed Dressing

½	cup sugar
2	teaspoons flour
2	teaspoons paprika
⅓	cup cider vinegar
1	cup salad oil
1	tablespoon lemon juice
1½	teaspoons poppy seeds

Combine sugar, flour, paprika and vinegar in a saucepan, bring to a boil, continue boiling 1 minute. Pour into a food processor or blender. With machine running, add oil in a thin stream until thoroughly incorporated. If added too fast, sauce may separate. Add lemon juice and poppy seeds, using an on-and-off technique to thoroughly blend in seeds. Refrigerate until ready to use.

1½ cups

Kit's mother often served this over grapefruit, orange and avocado slices for bridge luncheons in Mexico. It has become a favorite at the Mansion.

FROM THE GARDEN

Broccoli with Pine Nuts and Capers

3	pounds fresh broccoli
⅓	cup butter
⅓	cup pine nuts
2	garlic cloves, minced
½	cup water
3	tablespoons capers, well drained
	Salt and freshly ground pepper to taste

Remove and separate broccoli flowerets from stems. Peel stems, halve lengthwise if thick, cut crosswise into ½-inch slices. (Yield should be 8 cups flowerets and stems.) Drop broccoli into a 4-quart saucepan filled with boiling salted water, cook 4 minutes. Rinse under cold water, drain and pat dry.

Melt butter in a large skillet, add pine nuts and garlic. Sauté 30 seconds, remove mixture, set aside. Add broccoli to skillet, toss over moderate heat for 2 minutes. Add water, cover, cook over high heat for 6 minutes or until tender-crisp. Add pine nut mixture and capers, season with salt and pepper. Cook uncovered over high heat 1 minute. Taste and adjust seasoning. Serve hot.

8 to 10 servings

Fresh broccoli is available year-round at reasonable prices in most markets and is far superior to the frozen.

Carrots Cointreau

A glamorous companion for any green vegetable.

30	fresh baby carrots, cooked
2	tablespoons orange-flavored liqueur
¼	cup brandy
¼	cup honey
1½	tablespoons lemon juice
	Chopped parsley

Preheat oven to 350°.

Place carrots in a buttered shallow 1½ quart baking dish. In a bowl, combine remaining ingredients, except parsley, mix well, pour over carrots. Sprinkle with parsley. Bake 15 minutes or until thoroughly heated.

Note: Frozen baby carrots may be substituted; cook according to package directions.

6 servings

Souffléed Corn

There is no greater summer treat than succulent kernels of Missouri corn freshly picked from the field and quickly cooked.

6	ears of corn
¾	cup butter, divided
½	cup sugar, divided
1	tablespoon flour
1½	teaspoons baking powder
½	cup evaporated milk
2	eggs, well beaten
1	teaspoon cinnamon

Preheat oven to 350°.

Cut corn kernels from cobs.

Melt ½ cup of butter. Stir in ¼ cup sugar, gradually add flour and baking powder. Blend in milk and eggs, add corn, mix well. Pour into a greased 8-inch round baking dish.

Bake 35 minutes or until done. Remove from oven. Melt remaining butter, combine with remaining sugar and the cinnamon. Brush top of soufflé with mixture while still hot.

6 to 8 servings

Sautéed Cucumbers

8	cucumbers, peeled
3	tablespoons white wine vinegar
2	teaspoons salt
¼	teaspoon sugar
3	tablespoons minced shallots
4	tablespoons butter
	Salt and freshly ground pepper to taste
¼	cup chopped parsley

Cut cucumbers in half lengthwise. Scoop out seeds, cut into ½-inch strips lengthwise and cut strips into 2-inch pieces. Place in a bowl, toss with vinegar, salt and sugar, let stand at least 20 minutes.

Sauté shallots in butter until soft. Drain cucumbers and pat dry, add to shallots and toss until tender-crisp. Season with salt and pepper, add parsley, toss lightly. Taste and adjust seasoning. Serve in a clear glass dish.

8 servings

Although usually eaten raw, cucumbers make a marvelous hot vegetable dressed with either parsley or dill. Excellent with salmon, trout or poached chicken.

Eggplant and Pepper Gratin

A wonderful, colorful way to enjoy your garden's bounty. Red peppers (fully matured green peppers) are most plentiful in the early fall. They give added flavor and sweetness to this dish, which may be served warm or at room temperature.

3	medium eggplants, unpeeled with skin scored lengthwise in quarters, cut crosswise into ¼-inch slices
	Salt
6	large peppers, sweet red and green
1	cup oil, divided
3	tablespoons pine nuts
¾	cup fresh bread crumbs
	Cracked pepper to taste
	Pinch of orégano
3	tablespoons chopped fresh parsley
2	tablespoons capers
1	4-ounce jar whole pimientos, seeded and cut into strips
½	cup black olives, preferably Greek, halved and pitted

Preheat broiler.

Place eggplant in a colander, sprinkle with salt, drain 1 hour. Brush peppers with oil, place on a cookie sheet under broiler, turn until well-scorched. Rinse under cold water, remove skins. Halve peppers, remove seeds and cut into thick strips, set aside.

Heat 2 tablespoons of oil, add pine nuts, sauté until brown. Add bread crumbs, sauté briefly. Season with cracked pepper, orégano, parsley and a pinch of salt. Remove from heat.

Drain eggplant, pat dry. Brush slices with oil on both sides. Broil, turning once, until brown.

Preheat oven to 350°.

In an oval 2-quart baking dish, layer ½ of the eggplant, top with ½ of the peppers. Sprinkle with capers, repeat layers. Cover with bread crumb mixture. Arrange pimiento strips in a spoke pattern with olives in center, drizzle with tablespoons oil. Bake 15 minutes or until warm.

4 to 6 servings

*Restored Double Parlor,
dedicated August 20,
1983, will feature a
Wilton carpet loomed in
England in an 1869
pattern.*

Marbleized Corinthian column and stenciled ceiling detail of the Double Parlor.

Eggplant with Ginger and Sesame Seeds

1	2-pound eggplant, peeled and cut into ¾-inch cubes
½	cup sesame seeds
4	scallions, thinly sliced
1	tablespoon peeled and grated fresh ginger
½	teaspoon salt
3	tablespoons sesame oil
2	teaspoons lime juice
	Chopped parsley

Preheat oven to 350°.

Boil eggplant in lightly salted water 3 to 4 minutes or until barely tender, drain well.

Spread sesame seeds on a baking sheet, toast until lightly browned. Place in a food processor or blender, process to a smooth paste. Transfer to a bowl and combine with scallions, ginger and salt.

Sauté eggplant in oil over moderately high heat for 5 minutes, tossing frequently. Add sesame seed mixture, sauté 2 minutes or until heated through. Stir in lime juice, sprinkle with chopped parsley. Serve hot or cold.

6 servings

Akin to zucchini in its versatility, the beautiful purple eggplant originated in China and India. You'll like this exotic combination of flavors—sesame, ginger and eggplant.

Curried Vegetable Ragoût

Do not let the length of this recipe deter you! Appealing served in eggplant shells and garnished with pimiento strips, black olives and green pepper slices.

1	medium eggplant, unpeeled and cut into 1-inch cubes
2	medium zucchini, cut into 1-inch cubes
	Salt and freshly ground pepper to taste
8	tablespoons vegetable oil, divided
1	hot dried chili pepper, broken into 3 pieces, or 1 teaspoon crushed dried red pepper
2	cups finely sliced onions
2	large garlic cloves, minced
1	large green pepper, seeded and finely sliced
4	large ripe tomatoes, peeled, seeded and chopped
½	cup finely sliced pimientos
1½	teaspoons curry powder, or to taste
1	cup uncooked long-grain rice
1¼	cups water or chicken broth

Place eggplant and zucchini in colanders, salt, drain 30 minutes, pat dry.

Heat 4 tablespoons of oil in a large skillet, add eggplant, cook until brown. Remove eggplant, set aside. Add 2 tablespoons oil to skillet, repeat with zucchini.

Add 2 tablespoons oil to skillet, sauté chili pepper, onion and garlic until soft but not brown. Add green pepper, tomatoes and pimientos. Season with salt and pepper. Bring to a boil, cook uncovered until juices have evaporated.

Add zucchini and eggplant, cook 3 minutes. Stir in curry, rice and water (broth), bring to a boil. Reduce heat, cover simmer 30 minutes or until broth is absorbed and rice is tender.

Remove pieces of chili pepper, discard. Serve ragoût at room temperature.

Note: One 28-ounce can Italian plum tomatoes may be substituted for fresh tomatoes.

10 servings

Ratatouille Catalan

3	tablespoons vegetable oil
2	medium onions, chopped
4	garlic cloves, crushed
2	medium eggplants, cut into ¾-inch cubes
1	green pepper, seeded and cut into ½-inch pieces
1	sweet red pepper, seeded and cut into ½-inch pieces
8	ripe tomatoes, peeled, seeded and chopped
6	medium zucchini, sliced ½-inch thick
3	tablespoons chopped fresh parsley
2	teaspoons salt
	Cracked pepper to taste
¼	teaspoon thyme
½	teaspoon basil
2	bay leaves
½	cup water

Prepare ratatouille the day before serving.

Heat oil in a large skillet, sauté onion and garlic over low heat for 5 minutes. Add remaining ingredients, mix well. Cover, simmer 45 minutes, stirring occasionally. (Check after 30 minutes. If watery, cook uncovered until liquid is absorbed.) Zucchini should be slightly crunchy. Remove bay leaves, discard. Taste and adjust seasoning.

Serve warm or cold with lemon slices as a first course. Garnish with grated cheese.

Note: Two 28-ounce cans Italian plum tomatoes may be substituted for fresh tomatoes. Drain, reserving liquid for use in place of water in recipe.

12 to 16 servings

A kaleidoscope of summer vegetables. Wonderful served at room temperature with grilled lamb, beef or chicken. For a light luncheon entrée, sprinkle with freshly grated Parmesan and warm thoroughly.

Pattypan Squash with Puréed Peas

Testimony that eye-appeal and unusual presentation are important factors in successful menus. As an alternative to the puréed peas, substitute Hollandaise sauce.

8	small pattypan (cymling) squash
1	10-ounce package frozen peas
4	tablespoons unsalted butter, melted
2	tablespoons heavy cream, warmed
	Salt and freshly ground pepper to taste
	Fine bread crumbs
	Butter
	Freshly grated Parmesan cheese

Preheat oven to 350°.

Drop whole squash in boiling water, cook until barely tender when pierced with a fork. Squash should still be firm. When cool, remove stem and hollow out center of squash, using a paring knife to cut a circle and a grapefruit spoon to carefully remove seeds and pulp. Caution: Do not cut through sides or bottom. Invert on paper towels to drain.

Cook peas until barely done, drain in a colander. Place in a food processor or blender with melted butter and cream, season with salt and pepper, purée. Taste and adjust seasoning.

Fill squash with purée. Sprinkle lightly with bread crumbs. Dot with a thin slice of butter, sprinkle with cheese. Place in a baking pan coated with vegetable spray, bake 15 minutes.

Preheat broiler.

Place under broiler to brown. Serve immediately.

Note: Small yellow squash may be substituted for pattypan squash.

8 servings

Zucchini and Cherry Tomatoes

4	to 6 6-inch zucchini
¼	cup butter
¼	cup finely chopped onion
½	garlic clove, minced
¾	cup halved cherry tomatoes
	Salt and freshly ground pepper to taste
2	tablespoons sesame seeds, toasted
¼	cup finely chopped parsley

Slice zucchini on the bias into ½-inch slices. In a 4-quart pan of rapidly boiling water, blanch zucchini 1 minute. Rinse with cold water, drain, pat dry.

Melt butter, add onion and garlic, sauté until soft and golden brown. Add zucchini, cover, cook 2 minutes. Add tomatoes, cover, cook 1 minute. Season with salt and pepper, add sesame seeds and parsley. Toss, taste and adjust seasoning, serve.

6 servings

Red and green are, indeed, complementary colors.

Zucchini Parmesan

For vegetable lovers, the squash family is a bountiful blessing.

8	4- to 5-inch zucchini
2	tablespoons vegetable oil
	Salt and freshly ground pepper to taste
4	tablespoons butter
¼	pound Parmesan cheese, grated

Preheat oven to 350°.

Add zucchini and oil to a 4-quart pan of boiling water, parboil 10 minutes. Remove and drain.

Cut zucchini in half lengthwise. Place cut side up in a buttered 9 x 13-inch baking dish, season with salt and pepper, dot with butter. Cover with cheese. (Dish may be refrigerated at this point if preparing in advance. Bring to room temperature before baking.)

Bake 15 minutes or until heated through. Before serving, lightly brown cheese under preheated broiler.

6 to 8 servings

Cranberry-Orange Acorn Squash

4	small acorn squash, cut in half lengthwise and seeded
	Salt to taste
1	cup fresh cranberries, chopped
1	large orange, peeled and diced
2	tablespoons butter, melted
	Dark brown sugar

Preheat oven to 350°.

Place squash halves cut side down in a greased shallow baking dish, bake 25 minutes. Remove from oven, turn halves and sprinkle cavities with salt.

Mix cranberries, orange and butter and fill cavities. Bake 25 minutes or until squash is tender. Remove from oven, sprinkle lightly with brown sugar. Before serving, heat under preheated broiler until bubbly.

8 servings

The flavor of this popular winter squash is enhanced by the slightly tart cranberry-orange filling. A beautiful choice with Stuffed Roast of Pork or the traditional turkey and dressing.

Honeyed Brussels Sprouts

2	pints fresh Brussels sprouts
6	tablespoons butter, melted
6	tablespoons honey
1	garlic clove, crushed
	Salt and freshly ground pepper to taste

Cook sprouts in boiling salted water until tender-crisp, drain well and dry. Combine butter, honey and garlic in a saucepan, add sprouts, heat thoroughly. Season with salt and pepper. Taste and adjust seasoning.

8 servings ❧

Although available most of the year, this miniature member of the cabbage family is at its peak during the winter months. Brussels sprouts have a marvelous affinity for pork.

139

Spinach Ramekins

If you did not like spinach before, you will now! Delightful served cold, drizzled with oil and lemon juice.

½	cup minced green onions, including tops
5	tablespoons unsalted butter, divided
2	pounds fresh spinach leaves, cooked, drained and chopped
3	eggs, well beaten
3	egg yolks, well beaten
1½	cups light cream
¾	cup dry bread crumbs
¼	teaspoon freshly ground white pepper
¼	cup plus 1 tablespoon grated Parmesan cheese
1	teaspoon salt
⅛	teaspoon freshly grated nutmeg
8	to 10 large mushroom caps, fluted

Preheat oven to 350°.

Butter 8 or 10 6-ounce ramekins, cut wax paper to fit bottoms, butter paper. Sauté green onions in 3 tablespoons of butter for 5 minutes until soft. Combine all ingredients, except mushrooms and remaining butter, mix well. Spoon mixture into prepared ramekins.

Place ramekins in a large baking dish containing 1 inch hot water. Bake 20 to 30 minutes or until a knife inserted between center and side of ramekin comes out clean.

Sauté mushroom caps for 5 minutes in remaining butter until golden brown. Unmold ramekins, remove wax paper. Top with mushroom caps and serve.

8 to 10 servings

Red Cabbage with Apples

2	to 2½ pounds red cabbage
⅔	cup red wine vinegar
2	tablespoons sugar
2	teaspoons salt
2	tablespoons bacon fat
2	medium cooking apples, peeled, cored and cut into ⅛-inch-thick wedges
½	cup finely chopped onion
1	whole onion, peeled and pierced with 2 cloves
1	small bay leaf
5	cups boiling water
3	tablespoons dry red wine
3	tablespoons currant jelly

Wash cabbage and remove tough outer leaves. Cut into quarters and shred into ⅛-inch-wide strips. Combine cabbage, vinegar, sugar and salt, toss well, set aside.

In a 4- to 5-quart Dutch oven, melt bacon fat over moderate heat. Add apples and chopped onion, cook 5 minutes or until apples are golden brown, stirring frequently. Add cabbage, whole onion and bay leaf, mix well.

Pour in boiling water, bring to a boil over high heat, stirring occasionally. Reduce heat to lowest point, cover, simmer 1½ to 2 hours until tender. (If cabbage dries out while cooking, add small amount of boiling water.) Remove from heat, drain.

Just before serving, remove onion and bay leaf, discard. Stir in wine and currant jelly.

6 to 8 servings

Popular in Austria and Hungary, red cabbage is excellent both raw as a salad and cooked. Combined with the apples, it is a savory salute to the game season. Especially nice with duck and goose.

Skillet Glazed Onions

Our Thanksgiving turkey is always accompanied by this easy, elegant dish. A food processor is a real help in slicing the onions.

¼	cup butter
2	teaspoons vegetable oil
8	large Bermuda onions, thinly sliced
2	teaspoons salt
½	teaspoon freshly ground pepper
¼	cup plus 2 tablespoons packed brown sugar

Heat butter and oil in a large cast-iron skillet, add onions, sauté 10 minutes or until they begin to brown. Reduce heat, stir in salt and pepper. Cook partially covered, stirring frequently, until onions are very soft and turn a caramel color, about 30 minutes. Add sugar, stir until dissolved. Serve with game or fowl.

8 to 10 servings

Lemon Yam Puff

A scrumptious way to serve an edible root--the yam or sweet potato.

4	pounds yams
1	cup packed brown sugar
½	cup butter, softened
½	teaspoon salt
2	teaspoons grated orange rind
2	teaspoons grated lemon rind

Preheat oven to 350°.

Cook unpeeled whole sweet potatoes in boiling water for 30 minutes or until tender, drain, reserve liquid. Peel potatoes and mash until smooth. (If mixture seems dry, add some reserved liquid.

Add remaining ingredients and beat until light and fluffy. Transfer to greased 2-quart casserole, bake 30 minutes. Serve hot.

8 to 10 servings.

Swiss Potato Gratin

2	pounds red-skinned boiling potatoes, peeled
1	cup ricotta cheese
¾	cup chopped parsley
	Salt and freshly ground pepper to taste
	Nutmeg to taste
1	egg, lightly beaten
1	cup heavy cream
¼	pound Grùyere cheese, grated

Preheat oven to 350°.

Slice potatoes thinly into a pot of heavily salted cold water. Bring to a boil, cook 1 minute. Transfer to a colander, rinse with cold water, pat dry.

Combine ricotta and parsley, season generously with salt, pepper and nutmeg, set aside. Combine egg and enough cream to make 1 cup, set aside.

In a lightly buttered 9 x 12-inch oval gratin dish, arrange ¼ of the potato slices in an overlapping pattern, dot with ⅓ of the ricotta mixture, sprinkle with ⅓ of the Grùyere. Arrange two more layers in the same order. Top with layer of remaining potatoes. Pour egg and cream mixture into the dish, making sure cream spreads throughout layers.

Bake on center rack for 35 to 45 minutes, or until potatoes are tender and cheese is browned and bubbling. Let stand 10 minutes before serving. Garnish with sprigs of fresh parsley.

5 servings

Guaranteed to please the "meat and potato" members of your family. A perfect selection for a pot-luck supper or a dinner party.

FROM THE SIDEBOARD

Curried Chicken Salad

2	cups diced cooked chicken breast
4	scallions, sliced
1	cup sliced water chestnuts
2	cups cooked rice, at room temperature
1	cup mayonnaise
½	cup prepared chutney
1	teaspoon curry powder, or to taste
1	teaspoon salt
	Freshly ground pepper to taste
2	bananas
¼	cup lemon juice
1½	cups chopped peanuts

Combine chicken, scallions and water chestnuts with rice. In a separate bowl, combine mayonnaise, chutney, curry, salt and pepper, mix well. Thoroughly combine mayonnaise dressing with chicken-rice mixture, chill. Taste and adjust seasoning.

Cut bananas diagonally into 1-inch slices. Dip into lemon juice and coat with peanuts. To serve, arrange salad on small platter. Surround salad with banana slices and garnish with chopped nuts.

Note: Additional condiments may be served—chopped green peppers, toasted almonds, plumped raisins and coconut are a few choices.

6 to 8 servings

Our choice for Samuel's christening luncheon on Father's Day, 1982. Pass Cold Cucumber Soup on trays and serve the salad on the sideboard with Asparagus Vinaigrette and a watermelon basket of strawberries and assorted melon balls.

Chicken Pasta Primavera

This delicious entrée salad is glorious to behold and well suited for informal summertime entertaining.

1	tablespoon vegetable oil
¾	pound uncooked fettuccine, preferably freshly made
1	bunch broccoli, separated into flowerets
2	medium zucchini, cut into ¼-inch slices
1	bunch scallions, thinly sliced
1	sweet red pepper, cut into 1-inch slices
1	6-ounce can pitted black olives, drained and sliced
1	2-ounce jar pimientos, drained and sliced
2	cups cubed cooked chicken breast
	Basil Sauce
⅔	cup freshly grated Parmesan cheese, divided
	Salt and freshly ground pepper to taste

Add oil to 3 quarts boiling salted water. Cook fresh pasta 2 to 3 minutes (if packaged is used, cook 8 to 10 minutes), stirring occasionally. Caution: Do not overcook. Rinse with cold water, drain.

Combine vegetables and chicken with pasta. Fold in ⅔ of the Basil Sauce and ½ cup cheese. Season with salt and pepper. (Dish may now be refrigerated for 24 hours.)

To serve, add remaining Basil Sauce, taste and adjust seasoning and sprinkle with remaining cheese.

BASIL SAUCE:

¼	cup minced fresh basil
1	garlic clove
2	eggs
½	teaspoon dry mustard
1	tablespoon tarragon vinegar
½	teaspoon lemon juice
½	teaspoon salt
1½	cups vegetable oil
½	cup sour cream

Basil Sauce may be prepared in advance.

Place basil and garlic in a food processor or blender, process until minced. Add eggs, mustard, vinegar, lemon juice and salt, mix well. With machine running, add oil in a thin stream until thoroughly incorporated. If added too fast, sauce may separate. Caution: Use only enough oil to produce a medium-thick mayonnaise. Add sour cream, process 2 or 3 seconds. Refrigerate until ready to use.

8 servings

Beef and Avocado Salad

2	avocados, peeled and sliced
2	pounds very rare roast beef, thinly sliced
1	sweet red onion, thinly sliced
¾	cup vegetable oil
½	cup wine vinegar
2	teaspoons Dijon mustard
2	teaspoons salt
¼	teaspoon freshly ground pepper
	Chopped parsley

In a casserole, layer ½ of the avocado, ½ of the beef and ½ of the onion. Repeat with remaining avocados, beef and onion, set aside.

Mix remaining ingredients, except parsley, pour over layers. Cover, marinate 2 hours at room temperature, drain well, refrigerate. To serve, return to room temperature, arrange on a bed of Bibb or leafy red lettuce and sprinkle with parsley.

6 servings

Cold Roast Beef Salad

½	cup chopped sweet gherkins
2	bunches radishes, sliced
2	cups sliced fresh mushrooms
2	cups thinly sliced very rare roast beef
2	tablespoons drained capers
4	cups mixed greens, in bite-size pieces

SOUR CREAM DRESSING:

2	teaspoons Dijon mustard
¼	cup fresh lemon juice
2	tablespoons prepared horseradish
1	cup sour cream
6	tablespoons salad oil
¼	cup freshly grated Parmesan cheese
	Salt and freshly ground pepper to taste

Mix all ingredients, set aside.

Place mustard, lemon juice and horse-radish in a food processor or blender, mix well. Add sour cream, blend. With machine running, add oil in a thin stream until thoroughly incorporated. Add cheese, season with salt and pepper, mix. Taste and adjust seasoning.

Pour dressing over salad, toss well. Serve on chilled plates.

6 servings

Substantial and sensational!

Bavarian Sausage Salad

4	German knockwursts
½	tablespoon cider vinegar
½	teaspoon sugar
5	tablespoons vegetable oil
1	small red onion, thinly sliced
1	tablespoon drained capers
2	tablespoons finely chopped pimiento
1	small green pepper, diced
1	small dill pickle, thinly sliced
4	ripe tomatoes, quartered
	Salt and freshly ground pepper to taste
1	to 2 tablespoons minced parsley

Cook knockwursts 5 minutes in rapidly boiling water, drain, cool. Remove and discard skin. Cut sausages in thin slices, set aside.

Combine vinegar, sugar and oil in a glass or enamel container, whisk until sugar dissolves. Add knockwursts, onion, capers, pimiento, green pepper, pickle and tomatoes. Season with salt and pepper, toss lightly, refrigerate 2 to 4 hours. Taste and adjust seasoning. Sprinkle with parsley and serve chilled, but not cold.

6 to 8 servings

Ham Mousse

4	cups ground cooked ham
1	large onion, diced
½	cup golden raisins
2	to 3 tablespoons dry sherry or Madeira
1	teaspoon prepared horseradish
½	teaspoon nutmeg
2	teaspoons Dijon mustard
2	tablespoons unflavored gelatin
2	tablespoons cold water
1	cup chicken stock
1	cup heavy cream, whipped
2	tablespoons finely chopped fresh parsley

Combine ham, onion and raisins in a food processor, purée, or put through the finest blade of a meat grinder 3 times. Combine meat mixture, sherry (Madeira), horseradish, nutmeg and mustard, set aside.

Soften gelatin in cold water for 5 minutes. Bring chicken stock to a boil, add gelatin, stir over medium heat until dissolved. Add to ham mixture, blend thoroughly. Cool 10 to 15 minutes. Fold whipped cream and parsley into mixture.

Turn into a well-oiled 5-cup mold. Chill 3 hours or until firm. Unmold on a plate, garnish with sweet gherkins or stuffed green olives. Serve with very thin slices of French or rye bread.

Note: Because of its richness, serve the mousse in small portions when using as an entrée.

16 to 20 servings

There is no spectacle quite like the colors of changing autumn leaves. Pay homage to the season by planning a picnic in the woods. Include a spicy mustard sauce for the Ham Mousse, assorted cheeses, a basket of fruit and some chilled apple cider.

Salmon Mousse

Especially appealing
in a fish-shaped mold.
Glamourize this
buffet fare with
Cucumber Dill
Sauce.

2	16-ounce cans red salmon, drained
1	medium cucumber, peeled and cut into pieces
½	cup chopped onion
4	ribs celery, cut into pieces
	Few sprigs parsley, stemmed
	Juice of 1 lemon
3	tablespoons unflavored gelatin
1	10 ½-ounce can tomato soup
1	tablespoon chopped fresh basil
1	tablespoon chopped fresh chives
1	tablespoon chopped fresh parsley
1	8-ounce plus 1 3-ounce package of cream cheese, softened
1	cup mayonnaise
	Salt and freshly ground pepper to taste

Remove and discard salmon bones and skin, flake. Place cucumber, onion, celery and parsley in a food processor or blender, purée. Strain vegetables. Set aside liquid and puréed vegetables in separate bowls.

Combine vegetable liquid with lemon juice. Add gelatin, let soften 5 minutes. Heat tomato soup, add basil, chives, parsley and softened gelatin. Stir over medium heat until gelatin dissolves. Remove from heat, cool.

Combine salmon, cream cheese, mayonnaise, puréed vegetables and soup mixture, season with salt and pepper. Taste and adjust seasoning. Pour into a well-oiled 8-cup mold or individual molds, refrigerate overnight. Unmold and garnish with thinly sliced cucumbers, lemon wedges and watercress. Serve with Melba toast.

Note: Mousse improves in flavor if refrigerated an additional 24 hours.

8 cups

Carbonnade of Beef

2	tablespoons unsalted butter
2	tablespoons bacon fat
3	pounds boneless top sirloin, cut into ½-inch slices
	Salt and freshly ground pepper to taste
1½	pounds yellow onions, sliced
2	garlic cloves, minced
1	12-ounce can beer
1	cup beef stock
1	tablespoon brown sugar
5	to 6 sprigs parsley
1	bay leaf
1	teaspoon thyme
2	tablespoons cornstarch
2	tablespoons red wine vinegar

Preheat oven to 350°.

Heat butter and bacon fat together until sizzling. Brown meat a few slices at a time. Remove to a platter, season with salt and pepper. Brown remaining meat in the same manner, season, set aside.

Reduce heat, add onions, cook until brown. Transfer to a bowl, season with salt and pepper, stir in garlic.

Layer beef and onions in a 3-quart casserole. Combine beer, beef stock and brown sugar, mix well, pour into casserole. Tie parsley, bay leaf and thyme in a cheesecloth bag, add to casserole.

Bake covered for 2½ hours or until meat is tender. Discard cheesecloth bag. Pour liquid from casserole into a saucepan. Combine cornstarch and vinegar, add to liquid. Cook over medium heat, stirring constantly, until thickened. Taste and adjust seasoning. Serve sauce with meat. Garnish with chopped green onion tops and serve with boiled potatoes.

6 to 8 servings

An elegant choice for a dinner party. Serve Frosted Tomato Bisque for the first course and Chocolate Amaretto Mousse for dessert.

Mansion Moussaka

The classic Greek version is, of course, made with lamb, but beef is frequently substituted at the Mansion. Moussaka is ideal for make-ahead entertaining or a pot-luck supper. Serve with warm pita bread and a salad of romaine, chunks of feta cheese and Greek olives for a memorable meal.

3	medium eggplants, peeled and cut into ½-inch slices
1	cup butter, divided
3	large onions, finely chopped
2	pounds lamb or beef, ground
3	tablespoons tomato paste
½	cup red wine
½	cup chopped parsley
¼	teaspoon cinnamon
	Salt and freshly ground pepper to taste
6	tablespoons flour
1	quart milk
4	eggs, beaten
	Nutmeg to taste
2	cups ricotta or cottage cheese
1	cup fine bread crumbs, divided
1	cup freshly grated Parmesan cheese, divided

Preheat oven to 375°.

In a skillet, melt ¼ cup of butter, brown eggplant quickly, set aside. Melt ¼ cup of butter in same skillet. Sauté onions until brown, add meat, cook 10 minutes. Add tomato paste, wine, parsley and cinnamon, season with salt and pepper, mix well. Simmer, stirring frequently, until all liquid evaporates. Taste and adjust seasoning, remove from heat.

In a saucepan, melt remaining butter, whisk in flour. In another saucepan, bring milk to a boil and gradually add to sauce base, stirring constantly, until thickened and smooth. Remove from heat, cool slightly. Stir in eggs, nutmeg and ricotta cheese (cottage cheese), set aside.

Grease a 12 x 18-inch baking dish, dust the bottom with crumbs. Layer ½ of the eggplant, sprinkle with crumbs and cheese, layer ½ of the meat, sprinkle with crumbs and cheese. Repeat in the same order. Pour sauce evenly over top, bake 1 hour or until golden. Remove from the oven, let stand 25 minutes.

10 servings

Chicken Bombay

6	tablespoons butter
½	teaspoon paprika
1¼	teaspoons curry powder, or to taste
4	whole chicken breasts, poached, skinned, boned and cut into 1-inch pieces
1	pint heavy cream
1¼	teaspoons cornstarch
¼	cup dry sherry
1	cup cooked rice
	Salt and freshly ground pepper to taste
3	ounces Swiss cheese, grated

Melt butter in a large skillet, add paprika and curry. Briefly sauté chicken, coating all sides with the seasoned butter, set aside.

Bring cream to a boil in a saucepan. Dissolve cornstarch in sherry, add to cream, stirring constantly until thickened and smooth. Fold in chicken and rice, season with salt and pepper. Taste and adjust seasoning.

Transfer to a 2-quart baking dish. Sprinkle cheese on the top and brown under a preheated broiler.

Note: Can be served with any or all of the following sambals—chopped peanuts, raisins, grated orange rind, chopped parsley, chopped onion, chutney and coconut.

6 to 8 servings

The sambals or condiments are traditional with curry dishes and they add a festive touch to the buffet table. We have served Chicken Bombay with fresh asparagus and a salad to three hundred people at the Mansion. For a luncheon, we sometimes serve it with steamed fresh broccoli and a Tomato Chutney-filled peach half.

Chicken Chalupas

Why not mix up pitchers of margaritas? Add guacamole, tortilla chips, meat-filled tacos and you're ready for a fiesta "South of the Border." A piñata is a natural for your centerpiece.

12	ounces Monterey Jack cheese, grated
12	ounces sharp cheddar cheese, grated
2	bunches green onions, tops only, chopped
2	10¾-ounce cans cream of chicken soup
1	4-ounce can green chilies, chopped
1	pint sour cream
1	cup pitted black olives, sliced
4	large whole chicken breasts, poached, skinned, boned and cut into 1-inch pieces
12	6-inch flour tortillas

Combine cheeses, reserve half for topping and half for filling. Divide green onion tops into two equal portions.

Combine ½ of the cheeses, ½ of the onion tops, soup, chilies, sour cream and olives. Set aside 1½ cups of this mixture for topping. Add chicken to the remainder for filling, mix well.

Put 3 heaping tablespoons of filling on each tortilla and roll. Place tortilla seam side down in a lightly oiled shallow baking dish. Arrange tortillas in a single layer, using two baking dishes if necessary.

Spread reserved topping mixture over tortillas. Cover with remaining cheeses and onion tops. Refrigerate overnight or freeze. (If frozen, defrost completely before baking.)

Preheat oven to 350°.

Bake uncovered 45 minutes. Let stand a few minutes before serving.

Note: This is ideal for a brunch because it must be made ahead.

8 to 10 servings

Mexicana Chicken

1	10¾-ounce can cream of chicken soup
1	10½-ounce can cream of celery soup
1	10¾-ounce can chicken broth
1	4-ounce can green chilies, diced
12	corn tortillas, broken into small pieces
3	cups chopped cooked chicken
8	ounces cheddar cheese, grated

Preheat oven to 350°.

Combine soups, broth, chilies and tortillas, let stand 30 minutes. Place ½ of the mixture in a greased 9 x 13-inch baking dish. Cover with chicken, pour remaining mixture over chicken and sprinkle with cheese.

Bake uncovered 25 minutes.

8 to 10 servings

Add variety to family meals with this tasty chicken dish that children eat without coaxing.

Curried Chicken Crêpes

A staple for both buffet luncheons and dinners at the Mansion. Serve with sambals for added pizzazz.

2	tablespoons butter
1	cup chopped onions
2	tablespoons flour
½	teaspoon sugar
½	teaspoon salt
1	tablespoon curry powder, or to taste
1	cup chicken broth
1	cup light cream
3	cups diced cooked chicken
14	crêpes (see index)

Preheat oven to 350°.

Melt butter over medium heat in a large skillet. Add onions, sauté until golden. Stir in flour, sugar, salt and curry powder, mix well. Gradually add broth, then cream. Cook, stirring constantly, until thickened. Gently fold in chicken.

Put ¼ cup mixture in center of each crêpe and roll. Place crêpes seam side down in lightly oiled 9 x 13-inch baking dish.

CURRY SAUCE:

3	tablespoons butter
3	tablespoons flour
2	teaspoons curry powder, or to taste
½	teaspoon salt
	Dash Tabasco sauce
½	cup chicken broth
1	cup light cream
¼	cup chopped parsley
¼	cup cognac (optional)

Melt butter over medium heat in saucepan. Add flour, curry powder and salt, cook 2 to 3 minutes. Add Tabasco. Gradually add broth, then cream. Cook, stirring constantly, until thickened. Add parsley and cognac, pour over crêpes.

Bake uncovered 20 minutes or until sauce is bubbly.

Note: A 3- to 3½-pound chicken makes 3 cups diced meat.

6 to 8 servings

Crêpes Cannelloni

2	tablespoons vegetable oil
¾	cup minced onion
1	garlic clove, minced
1½	pounds ground chuck
1	cup chopped drained cooked spinach
1	egg, lightly beaten
¼	cup grated Parmesan cheese
	Salt and freshly ground pepper to taste
4	tablespoons butter
4	tablespoons flour
2	cups milk
½	cup prepared spaghetti sauce
14	crêpes (see index)
1	6-ounce package sliced mozzarella cheese, cut into 1½ x 5-inch pieces

Preheat oven to 350°.

Heat oil in a large skillet. Sauté onions and garlic over medium heat until translucent, but not brown. Add beef and brown, stirring frequently, drain. Combine meat with spinach, egg and Parmesan cheese. Season with salt and pepper, taste and adjust seasoning. Reserve ¼ cup mixture for cream sauce.

Make the sauce by melting butter in a saucepan over medium heat, whisk in flour. Add milk, stirring constantly, until thickened and smooth. Stir in reserved meat mixture, simmer 5 minutes, season with salt and pepper. Taste and adjust seasoning.

Spread spaghetti sauce on bottom of greased 9 x 13-inch baking dish. Spread 2 tablespoons meat filling on each crêpe and roll. Place crêpe seam side down on spaghetti sauce. Spoon cream sauce over crêpes and top each with a slice of mozzarella cheese.

Bake uncovered 30 minutes or until thoroughly heated. Let stand briefly before serving.

8 to 10 servings

Artichoke Pie

1	9-inch pie shell, unbaked
1	9-ounce package frozen artichoke hearts, sliced
4	tablespoons butter
½	cup chopped onion
1	tablespoon flour
½	cup light cream
½	cup sour cream
4	eggs, beaten
¼	teaspoon nutmeg
2	teaspoons minced fresh parsley
	Salt and freshly ground pepper to taste
½	cup shredded cheddar cheese
½	cup shredded Swiss cheese
¼	cup freshly grated Parmesan cheese

Preheat oven to 350°.

Line a quiche pan or deep-dish pie plate with pie shell and flute edges. Cook artichoke hearts as directed on package, drain on paper towels, set aside.

Melt butter over medium heat in a large skillet. Sauté onions until tender, but not brown, about 5 minutes. Stir in flour, add cream. Cook 3 to 5 minutes, stirring constantly, until thickened.

Add sour cream, eggs, nutmeg and parsley. Season with salt and pepper, mix well, taste and adjust seasoning, set aside.

Layer ½ of the artichoke hearts in pie shell, sprinkle with cheddar cheese, repeat artichoke layer, sprinkle with Swiss cheese. Pour sauce over layers, sprinkle with Parmesan cheese. Bake 45 minutes, serve immediately.

4 to 6 servings

A member of the thistle family, the artichoke is one of the oldest foods known to man. This popular vegetable is showcased in a savory custard pie.

Eggs Florentine

Eggs and spinach invariably result in a happy union, and this colorful dish is no exception. A typical brunch menu at the Mansion might feature Eggs Florentine and include Glazed Canadian Bacon, Kentucky Cheese Grits and large crystal bowls filled with fresh strawberries and powdered sugar for dipping.

10	slices bacon, diced
9	tablespoons butter, divided
1	6-ounce can sliced mushrooms, drained, divided
½	cup plus 2 tablespoons flour
	Salt and freshly ground pepper to taste
5	cups milk
2	10-ounce packages frozen chopped spinach, thawed and squeezed dry
¼	teaspoon nutmeg
2	dozen eggs, beaten
1¼	cups evaporated milk

Preheat oven to 275°.

In a skillet, sauté bacon until golden, drain on paper towels, reserve ¼ cup. Pour off bacon grease. Melt 4 tablespoons of butter in the skillet. Return remaining bacon and ⅔ of the mushrooms to pan. Add flour, season with salt and pepper, mix well. Gradually add milk, stirring constantly until sauce is thickened and smooth, set aside.

Combine spinach and nutmeg in a mixing bowl. Thoroughly blend in 2 cups of sauce mixture. Taste and adjust seasoning, set aside. Reserve remaining sauce.

In a large skillet, melt 5 tablespoons of butter over medium heat. Season eggs to taste, stir in evaporated milk. Scramble egg mixture until soft.

In a lightly greased 4-quart casserole layer ½ of the eggs, spinach mixture, remaining eggs and remaining sauce. Sprinkle top with reserved bacon and remaining mushrooms. Bake uncovered 1 hour. Serve immediately.

10 to 12 servings

Cheese and Eggs Olé

1	dozen eggs, beaten
½	cup flour
1	teaspoon baking powder
1	pint cottage cheese
1	pound Monterey Jack cheese, shredded
½	cup butter, melted
2	4-ounce cans green chiles, diced

Preheat oven to 350°.

Combine all ingredients. Pour into a buttered 9 x 13-inch baking dish. Bake 35 minutes or until done. Serve immediately.

8 to 10 servings

The green chilies add distinction to an easy and tasty brunch dish. Serve with bowls of salsa, guacamole and sour cream and a huge basket of crispy tortilla chips.

Quesadillas

1	pound block Monterey Jack cheese
1	pound block cheddar cheese
1	4-ounce can green chilies, chopped
1	large onion, chopped
12	9-inch flour tortillas
1	28-ounce can Italian plum tomatoes, chopped
2	to 3 tablespoons prepared jalapeño sauce
1	green pepper, sliced into rings

Preheat oven to 425°.

Slice each cheese into 12 equal lengthwise strips. Put a strip of each cheese, a spoonful of chilies and a spoonful of onion on a tortilla and roll.

Place tortillas seam side down in 2 lightly oiled 9 x 13-inch baking dishes. Mix tomatoes with jalapeño sauce, pour over tortillas. Top with green pepper slices. Bake uncovered 25 to 30 minutes.

6 to 8 servings

Tahoe Brunch

½	cup plus 3 tablespoons butter, divided
12	slices white bread, crusts removed
½	pound fresh mushrooms, trimmed and sliced
2	cups thinly sliced yellow onions
	Salt and freshly ground pepper
1½	pounds mild Italian sausage (if link sausage, remove casings)
¾	to 1 pound cheddar cheese, grated
5	eggs, beaten
2½	cups milk
3	teaspoons Dijon mustard
1	teaspoon dry mustard
1	teaspoon nutmeg
2	tablespoons minced fresh parsley

Soften 3 tablespoons of butter, spread on bread, set aside. Melt ½ cup of butter over medium heat in a large skillet. Sauté mushrooms and onions 5 to 8 minutes or until tender. Remove from skillet, season with salt and pepper, set aside.

In the same skillet, cook sausage over medium heat, about 20 minutes or until brown and cooked through. Drain and break into bite-size pieces.

In a greased 9 x 13-inch baking dish, layer ½ of the bread, mushroom mixture, sausage and cheese. Repeat layers in the same order.

Mix eggs, milk, mustards, nutmeg, 1 teaspoon salt and ⅛ teaspoon pepper. Pour over layers, refrigerate overnight.

Preheat oven to 350°.

Bake uncovered 1 hour or until bubbly. Sprinkle with parsley, serve immediately.

Note: For a milder version, substitute 1⅓ cups chopped scallions for yellow onions and sliced American cheese for cheddar cheese.

8 servings

According to an old saying, "In the morning it is best to dine like a king, at midday like a prince and in the evening like a pauper." Try this for a truly regal brunch.

French Bread Pizza

The star of any smorgasbord.

1	crusty loaf of French bread
3	tomatoes, peeled, seeded, and finely chopped
¼	to ½ cup vegetable oil
3	garlic cloves, minced
	Pinch of oregano
	Pinch of basil
	Salt and freshly ground pepper to taste
1	8-ounce package shredded mozzarella cheese

Preheat oven to 350°.

Cut bread in half lengthwise. Combine remaining ingredients, except cheese, mix well. Taste and adjust seasoning. Spread on cut side of each bread half, sprinkle cheese on top. Place on a cookie sheet, bake 10 to 15 minutes or until topping is bubbly.

6 servings

Tailgate Hero Sandwich

1	crusty loaf of French bread
	Prepared Italian dressing
	Mayonnaise
	Durkee sauce
⅓	pound smoked turkey, thinly sliced
⅓	pound corned beef, thinly sliced
⅓	pound ham, thinly sliced
⅓	pound baby Swiss cheese, thinly sliced
⅓	pound provolone cheese, thinly sliced
⅓	pound New York cheddar cheese, thinly sliced
2	medium tomatoes, thinly sliced and drained on paper towels
2	medium green peppers, thinly sliced into rings
1	red onion, thinly sliced and separated into rings

The sandwich may be prepared and refrigerated for up to 48 hours before serving.

Cut loaf in half lengthwise. Scoop out centers, leaving a ½-inch shell. Spread both halves with Italian dressing. Generously spread mayonnaise over one half and Durkee over the other.

Layer turkey, corned beef and ham on both halves, layer cheeses on meat, and tomatoes, green peppers and onion on cheeses.

Carefully put halves together. Wrap sandwich tightly with foil and refrigerate. To serve, cut into 1½- to 2-inch slices.

Note: Sliced avocados and alfalfa sprouts may be substituted for green peppers; add just before serving. Other meats may be substituted for those listed.

10 to 12 servings

Because it can be assembled one to two days in advance, this colossal sandwich is perfect for float trips, tailgates and family picnics. Featuring three meats, three cheeses and three vegetables, it qualifies as a meal in itself. Don't forget a generous supply of napkins!

Sausage Apple Ring

Sausage and apples do indeed go together. Team this winner with Eggs Florentine.

1½	cups dry fine bread crumbs
2	eggs, slightly beaten
½	cup buttermilk
2	pounds bulk sausage
½	cup minced onion
1	cup finely chopped peeled apple
2	teaspoons sage
1	cup brown sugar
1	teaspoon dry mustard
3	tablespoons vinegar

Preheat oven to 350°.

Place bread crumbs in a mixing bowl. Combine eggs and buttermilk, pour over bread crumbs, let stand 10 minutes or until liquid is absorbed. Add sausage, onion, apple and sage, mix well.

Firmly press mixture into a heavily greased 6-cup ring mold. Invert and unmold on rack in a broiler pan.

To make glaze, combine sugar, mustard and vinegar in a saucepan, heat.

Bake 1½ hours. After first hour, baste twice with glaze. To serve, fill sausage ring with scrambled eggs.

Note: It will take 4 pancake turners to successfully lift the sausage ring intact have someone ready to assist you.

8 servings

Glazed Canadian Bacon

¼	cup butter, melted
½	cup packed brown sugar
2	tablespoons grated orange rind
¼	cup orange juice
12	¼-inch-thick slices Canadian bacon

Preheat broiler.

Combine butter, brown sugar, orange rind and juice in a saucepan, bring to a boil. Remove from heat, cool.

Arrange bacon on a broiler pan. Brush each slice with glaze, place under broiler until lightly browned. Remove from broiler, turn slices, brush with glaze, return to broiler, brown lightly.

Note: Fast and easy meat dish. Sliced ham may be used instead of Canadian bacon.

6 servings

A popular brunch dish on the Mansion sideboard.

FROM THE PLATTER

Poached Salmon on the Grill

1	Coho or small Chinook salmon (8 to 15 pounds), cleaned
	Salt and freshly ground pepper
1	bunch fresh dill
1	bunch fresh parsley
2	to 3 lemons, thinly sliced
1	medium white onion, thinly sliced

Use a covered grill. When coals are ready, arrange them for indirect cooking (around sides of grill).

Generously salt and pepper stomach cavity of salmon. Layer remaining ingredients in cavity in following order: dill, parsley, lemon, onion, lemon, parsley and dill. Wrap stuffed salmon in heavy-duty aluminum foil, using a butcher's fold on top for easy opening.

Lay salmon on its side in middle of grill. With lid on, bake 65 to 85 minutes, depending on size of fish and heat of the coals.

The salmon is fully cooked when stomach cavity is hot to the touch. (If uncertain, check doneness by peeling skin back. Uncooked spots will vary in color.) Salmon is thoroughly cooked when it is a uniform light pink. Caution: Be careful not to overcook.

Remove stuffing from cavity; remove skin. Garnish with fresh watercress and lemon wedges.

Allow ½ pound of fresh salmon per serving

Following Kit's annual summer trek to Alaska for salmon fishing, our backyard grill gets a real workout. The Cucumber Dill Sauce is a must! I often serve Zucchini and Cherry Tomatoes as an accompaniment to the salmon. Crusty French bread and Blueberries with Lemon Mousse complete the meal.

Chicken Breasts with Cucumber

1	large cucumber, peeled, halved, seeded and cut into thin slices
½	cup chicken broth
½	cup dry white wine
6	whole chicken breasts, skinned, boned and halved
1½	teaspoons salt, divided
½	teaspoon pepper
3	tablespoons butter
½	cup cognac
⅓	cup thinly sliced scallions, white part only
1½	cups light cream
1	tablespoon grated lemon rind
2	tablespoons minced fresh parsley

Reserve ¾ of the cucumber slices. Combine remaining slices, broth and wine in a large saucepan. Bring to a boil, remove from heat, let stand 2 minutes. Strain, reserve liquid, discard cucumber.

Pound chicken until ½ inch thick. Sprinkle with ½ teaspoon of salt, season with pepper. Melt butter in a large skillet, sauté chicken 5 minutes. Warm cognac, pour over chicken, ignite. When flames subside, remove chicken to a plate, keep warm.

Add scallions to skillet, cover. Cook until tender but not brown. Return chicken to skillet, add reserved broth mixture. Cook covered 5 minutes over low heat. Transfer to platter, keep warm.

Over high heat, reduce liquid in skillet to ½ cup. Reduce heat, stir in cream, lemon rind and remaining salt. Simmer 3 to 4 minutes or until slightly thickened. Stir in reserved cucumber slices. To serve, pour sauce over chicken, sprinkle with parsley.

6 to 8 servings

Individual Beef Wellington

8	6-ounce beef fillets
	Vegetable oil
	Salt and freshly ground pepper to taste
¾	pound fresh mushrooms, chopped
4	tablespoons butter
¼	cup finely chopped scallions
1	teaspoon parsley
1	teaspoon chives
8	frozen patty shells, defrosted

Preheat oven to 450°.

Brush fillets with vegetable oil, season with salt and pepper. Heat heavy-bottomed skillet, sear fillets 5 minutes on each side. Cool on platter, chill.

To make duxelles, squeeze mushrooms in cheesecloth to extract moisture. Melt butter, stir in scallions, cook until soft. Add mushrooms, cook 10 to 15 minutes, stirring frequently, until moisture has evaporated and mushrooms are about to brown. Remove from heat, stir in parsley and chives. Season with salt and pepper.

Divide mushroom duxelles into 8 portions. Spread on fillets, chill.

Roll each patty shell out to a 9 x 5-inch rectangle. Place a chilled fillet on each rectangle with mushroom side down on dough. Fold dough over fillet, seal edges by pressing together. Place each pastry seam side down in a greased shallow baking pan. Bake 10 minutes for rare, 12 minutes for medium-rare and 15 minutes for medium. Serve with Beárnaise Sauce.

8 servings

The subtle flavor of the mushroom duxelles broadens the appeal and adds a new dimension to this elegant entrée.

Roast Beef Tenderloin

The ease of preparation helps balance budgetary considerations about this ever-popular cut of beef. Serve with a gravy boat of Béarnaise Sauce or Mustard Dill Sauce.

1	6-pound beef tenderloin
	Garlic
	Vegetable oil

Preheat oven to 450°.

Trim beef of fat and membrane, rub well with garlic and oil. Place meat on an oiled wire rack in a shallow pan, tucking narrow piece under for more uniform thickness. Using meat thermometer, roast 30 minutes or until temperature reaches 120°. Meat will be crusty brown outside and red inside. Let stand 5 minutes before carving.

8 servings

Standing Rib Roast

Throw away your meat thermometer! This cooking method insures nice rare slices in the center and crusty, well-done end pieces. Yorkshire Pudding is a traditional accompaniment.

1	standing rib roast, at least 4 pounds and two ribs thick
	Salt and freshly ground pepper to taste

ROASTING TIMETABLE:

4 to 5 pounds—30 minutes

6 pounds—42 minutes

More than 6 pounds— additional 12 minutes per pound

Preheat oven to 500°.

Beef must be at room temperature. Trim fat to a thin covering. Season well with salt and pepper. Roast uncovered, fat side down, for 30 minutes. Remove from oven, drain grease from roasting pan. Reduce temperature to 350°, roast according to timetable.

Remove roast from oven. Do not cover. Let stand for the same length of time roast was in oven. Roast may be reheated at 200° before serving.

Allow ½ pound per serving

Kansas City Kebabs

1½	pounds chuck beef, cut into 1½ inch cubes
	Unseasoned meat tenderizer
1	teaspoon dry mustard
½	teaspoon salt
¼	teaspoon orégano
½	teaspoon peppercorns
1	bay leaf
1	teaspoon minced onion
½	cup vegetable oil
1	cup beer
2	green peppers, cut into 1½-inch pieces
12	small whole onions
3	tomatoes, quartered
12	whole mushrooms

Place meat in a glass or enamelware container, sprinkle with tenderizer. Combine mustard, salt, orégano, peppercorns, bay leaf, onion, oil and beer, pour over beef. Refrigerate, marinate at least 5 hours, preferably overnight. Drain, reserving marinade.

Preheat broiler or prepare outdoor grill.

Arrange beef on skewers. On separate skewers, alternate vegetables grouped according to cooking time: green peppers with onions and tomatoes with mushrooms.

Place skewered vegetables 3 to 4 inches from source of heat. Cook 5 minutes, brushing with marinade and turning occasionally. Add skewered beef, cook 3 to 5 minutes, brushing frequently with marinade and turning after 2 minutes. Watch vegetables carefully and remove when done.

4 servings

Skewered foods—a marshmallow or a hot dog impaled on a stick—never lose their appeal to young and old alike. The secret to preparing skewered food is to group together items which have the same cooking times. The Rice and Mushroom Casserole is an ideal companion.

Butterflied Leg of Lamb

Another favorite of Kit's for outdoor barbecuing—the marinade is magical. Eggplant and Pepper Gratin or Curried Vegetable Ragoût and Tabbouleh are among my favorite offerings with lamb.

1	5- to 6-pound butterflied leg of lamb
1	cup vegetable oil
1	cup dry red wine
3	tablespoons red wine vinegar
2	tablespoons soy sauce
1	teaspoon rosemary
1	clove garlic, crushed
½	teaspoon salt
	Freshly ground pepper

Have the butcher butterfly the lamb (meat should be uniformly thick).

To make marinade, combine all ingredients, except lamb, mix well. Place meat in a glass or enamel container, pour marinade over lamb. Refrigerate at least 4 hours, preferably overnight, turning occasionally.

Using a covered grill, sear meat over hot coals. Arrange coals for indirect cooking (around sides of grill with a drip pan in the middle to catch meat drippings). Cook lamb until pink inside.

6 to 8 servings

Lamb Shanks with Chutney

4	lamb shanks
2	tablespoons vegetable oil
2	fresh tomatoes, peeled, seeded and chopped
2	teaspoons curry powder, or to taste
½	teaspoon ground ginger
1½	cups beef broth
½	teaspoon salt
1	clove garlic, minced
1	medium onion, finely chopped
½	cup prepared chutney
¾	cup uncooked rice
1	tablespoon minced fresh parsley

Brown lamb shanks in oil over medium-high heat for 5 minutes. Transfer to a 3-quart Dutch oven, set aside.

Place all ingredients, except rice and parsley, in a food processor or blender. Process 30 seconds or until mixed but not puréed, pour over lamb.

Place Dutch oven over medium-high heat and bring to a boil. Reduce heat, cover, simmer 2 hours.

Skim off fat, add rice and cover. Simmer 30 minutes or until rice is cooked. Sprinkle with parsley and garnish with chopped peanuts.

4 servings

The piquant flavor of the chutney elevates the lamb shanks to company cuisine.

Stuffed Roast of Pork

At a formal dinner party, perfection is the aim and nothing is more perfect for a winter menu than this beautiful Stuffed Roast of Pork. Either Cranberry-Orange Acorn Squash or Honeyed Brussels Sprouts are recommended for the vegetable course. For the finale—Maple Mousse with Rum Sauce.

¾	cup dry white wine
2	dozen pitted prunes
1	3½-to 4-pound boned loin of pork
	Salt and freshly ground white pepper to taste
5	to 8 tablespoons butter, divided
2	tablespoons vegetable oil
1	0.87-ounce package dry brown gravy mix
5	to 6 sprigs parsley
1	bay leaf
1	teaspoon thyme
¾	cup heavy cream
2	tablespoons currant jelly
1	teaspoon lemon juice
1	tablespoon cornstarch
1	teaspoon grated orange rind

Preheat oven to 375°.

Combine wine and prunes, marinate for 2 to 4 hours at room temperature. Cut a pocket into the center of the loin along the length of the roast to within 1 inch of each end. Stuff with 8 prunes, sew up pocket and tie string around roast in several places. Season with salt and pepper.

Melt 3 tablespoons butter in a Dutch oven, add oil. Brown meat well over medium heat, remove meat, set aside. Pour off all but 3 tablespoons fat from Dutch oven. (If fat is burned, discard and substitute 3 tablespoons butter.) Prepare gravy mix according to package directions, reserve 1 tablespoon, set aside. Add gravy to Dutch oven, bring to a boil. Drain wine from prunes and stir it into gravy mixture, bring to a boil.

Return meat to Dutch oven. Tie parsley, bay leaf and thyme in a cheese cloth bag, submerge in liquid. Cover place in oven and roast 2 hours or until meat is done.

Preheat broiler.

Remove meat from Dutch oven to a broiler pan. Discard cheesecloth bag, reserve meat juices. Broil meat 5 minutes. Caution: Watch meat carefully.

Thoroughly remove accumulated fat from meat juices. Place Dutch oven on burner, reduce liquid by ⅓ over high heat. Add cream and currant jelly, stirring constantly until jelly dissolves. Add lemon juice and remaining 16 prunes. Taste and adjust seasoning (sauce should have a sweet and sour taste). Mix cornstarch with reserved gravy, whisk into sauce. Cook, stirring, until sauce heavily coats spoon. Remove from heat, add 2 tablespoons butter and the orange rind.

Cut meat in thin slices. Carve only amount needed because pork tends to dry out. Serve with sauce.

to 8 servings ❦

Mandarin Pork Steaks

Suggested bill of fare with this favorite of backyard chefs: Summer Rice Salad, sliced home-grown tomatoes and Blueberry Peach Cobbler.

1	beef bouillon cube
⅓	cup hot water
1	teaspoon ground ginger
2	teaspoons salt
1	tablespoon sugar
¼	cup honey
¼	cup soy sauce
4	to 6 pork arm or blade steaks

Place bouillon and water in a lar[ge] glass, stainless steel or enamelwa[re] pan, stir until dissolved. Add all ingr[e] dients, except pork, mix well. A[dd] pork, refrigerate at least 2 hours, pr[e] ferably overnight, turning occasional[ly.]

Preheat oven to 350° or prepare ou[t] door grill.

Remove steaks from marinade a[nd] place on rack in shallow roasting pa[n.] Bake 50 minutes or until done, or gr[ill] 4 inches from coals 12 to 15 minut[es] on each side or until juices run clea[r.] Baste each side frequently with mari[n] ade.

4 to 6 servings

Governor's Stu[dy] second flo[or]

Living Room of First
Family quarters.

Breakfast on second-floor Porch.

Family Dining Room,
second floor.

Dove in Wine

20	dove breasts
	Salt and freshly ground pepper to taste
½	cup butter
1	cup dry white wine
1	carrot, diced
1	onion, chopped
3	tablespoons chopped celery
1	cup chopped mushrooms
3	slices blanched orange peel
2	tablespoons flour
2	cups chicken stock

Preheat oven to 350°.

Rub dove with salt and pepper. Melt butter in a large skillet over medium heat, add dove and brown. Remove to buttered 4-quart casserole. Pour wine over dove, cover.

In the same skillet, sauté carrot, onion, celery, mushrooms and orange peel for 5 minutes, stirring frequently. Add flour, mix. Gradually stir in stock. Cook until thickened.

Pour sauce over dove, cover. Bake 25 to 30 minutes or until tender. To serve, remove dove to warm platter, pass sauce.

6 servings

September 1 heralds the opening of dove season in Missouri, long a family ritual for Kit and his dad. A successful outing is followed by this specialty of the house. New England Baked Apples is a seasonal dessert choice.

Fourth of July celebration on the Mansion grounds with a vista of the Missouri River.

FOR THE FINALE

Chocolate Amaretto Mousse

1½	pounds semisweet chocolate chips
½	cup prepared espresso coffee
¼	cup Amaretto
4	egg yolks
2	cups heavy cream, chilled, divided
¼	cup sugar
8	egg whites
	Pinch of salt
½	teaspoon vanilla extract

Melt chocolate chips with coffee over simmering water in a double boiler. Stir in Amaretto, cool to room temperature. Add egg yolks, one at a time, beating thoroughly after each addition.

Whip 1 cup of cream until stiff, gradually adding sugar while beating. Beat egg whites with salt until stiff, fold into whipped cream. Stir ⅓ of cream mixture thoroughly into chocolate mixture. Gently fold in remaining cream mixture.

Pour into 8 individual dessert cups or a serving bowl. Refrigerate 2 hours or until set. At serving time, whip remaining cup of cream until soft peaks form, add vanilla. Top each portion with whipped cream and garnish with candied violets or chocolate shavings.

8 servings

The addition of the Amaretto provides a new dimension to a classic dessert.

Apple Mousse with Apricot Sauce

Fall is apple picking time in Missouri. Why not plan a dinner party featuring Mandarin Pork Steaks, Broccoli with Pine Nuts and Capers and Apple Mousse with Apricot Sauce? A caramel sauce also combines beautifully with the Apple Mousse.

MOUSSE:

4	medium apples, peeled, cored and quartered
½	teaspoon cinnamon
¼	cup apricot preserves
	Pinch of nutmeg
	Pinch of grated lemon rind
4	egg yolks
1	teaspoon cornstarch
¾	cup sugar
1½	cups warm milk
1	tablespoon unflavored gelatin
½	cup orange juice
1	teaspoon vanilla extract
1	cup heavy cream, whipped

Combine apples, cinnamon, preserves, nutmeg and lemon rind in a saucepan, cook until apples are soft and tender. Place in a food processor or blender, purée.

In a double boiler, beat egg yolks, cornstarch and sugar until mixture becomes fluffy and lemon colored. Add milk, cook over simmering water, stirring constantly, until custard coats the spoon. Caution: Do not allow to boil. Remove from heat.

In a heatproof measuring cup, soften gelatin in orange juice for 5 minutes. Place cup in simmering water and stir until gelatin dissolves. Stir into custard, chill 2 hours, stirring occasionally, until it starts to set.

Stir in vanilla and apple purée. Fold in whipped cream. Pour into a large crystal bowl or individual serving containers, chill 4 hours. Garnish with apple wedges and sprigs of mint. Serve with Apricot Sauce.

APRICOT SAUCE:

1	cup apricot preserves
2	tablespoons lemon juice
1	teaspoon grated lemon rind
¼	to ½ cup apricot brandy (to taste)
1½	to 2 tablespoons confectioners' sugar (to taste)
¼	cup kirsch

Heat preserves, lemon juice, lemon rind, brandy and sugar in a small saucepan, stir until preserves dissolve. Place sauce in a food processor or blender, purée. Add kirsch, adjust sugar and brandy to taste, chill.

8 to 10 servings

Lemon Mousse with Strawberry-Raspberry Sauce

MOUSSE:

4	eggs
3	eggs, separated
9	tablespoons sugar, divided
2	envelopes unflavored gelatin
3	tablespoons lemon juice
3	tablespoons water
	Grated rind of 1 lemon
¼	cup frozen lemonade concentrate, defrosted
2	cups heavy cream, whipped

Beat eggs, the 3 egg yolks and 6 tablespoons of sugar until thick and smooth. In a heatproof measuring cup, soften gelatin in lemon juice and water for 5 minutes. Place cup in simmering water and stir until gelatin dissolves, add to egg mixture with lemon rind and lemonade. Fold in whipped cream. Beat the 3 egg whites and remaining sugar until stiff peaks form, fold into mousse.

Pour into a straight-sided crystal bowl or an 8-inch soufflé dish which has had a lightly-oiled collar of wax paper tied or taped around the outside, extending 2 to 3 inches above the rim. Smooth top with a spatula, chill 6 hours or until firm. Remove collar and serve with Strawberry-Raspberry Sauce.

STRAWBERRY-RASPBERRY SAUCE:

1	10-ounce package sweetened frozen strawberries, defrosted
1	10-ounce package sweetened frozen raspberries, defrosted
2	teaspoons cornstarch
1	teaspoon water
1	teaspoon lemon juice
⅓	cup currant jelly
1	tablespoon kirsch
1	teaspoon Frambois

Place strawberries and raspberries in a food processor or blender, purée. Strain through a sieve lined with cheesecloth. Dissolve cornstarch in water. Combine purée and cornstarch in a saucepan, cook over low heat until mixture begins to thicken. Add lemon juice and jelly, stir until jelly dissolves. Remove from heat, cool. Blend in kirsch and Frambois, chill.

8 servings

Maple Mousse with Rum Sauce

A favorite of Kit's. I particularly like to serve this in the autumn following a dinner of pork, game or turkey.

MOUSSE:

1	envelope plus 2 teaspoons unflavored gelatin
½	cup cold water
1	cup pure maple syrup
4	eggs, separated
½	cup brown sugar
2	cups heavy cream, chilled

In a heatproof measuring cup, soften gelatin in cold water for 5 minutes. Place the cup in simmering water, stir until gelatin dissolves and is clear. Combine with maple syrup.

In a double boiler, beat egg yolks until thick and lemon colored. Add syrup mixture. Cook over simmering water, stirring constantly, until mixture heavily coats the spoon. Caution: Do not allow to boil. Remove from heat, stir in brown sugar. Pour into a large bowl, cool to room temperature.

Whip cream until soft peaks form, fold into maple mixture. Beat egg whites until stiff peaks form, fold into mousse until white no longer shows.

Rinse a 1½-quart mold in cold water, do not dry. Pour in mousse mixture, chill 4 hours or until firm. Unmold and serve with Rum Sauce.

RUM SAUCE:

1	cup milk
3	egg yolks
1	tablespoon sugar
2	tablespoons rum

Heat milk to boiling point, reduce heat. Combine egg yolks and sugar, add 2 tablespoons of milk, mix quickly. Repeat with 2 more tablespoons of milk. Over low heat, gradually whisk egg mixture into the milk. Caution: Sauce may separate if cooked at too high a temperature. Stir constantly until mixture lightly coats the spoon. Add rum, stir.

To serve, pour sauce over mousse.

8 servings

Orange Mousse with Grand Marnier Sauce

MOUSSE:

2	envelopes unflavored gelatin
1	cup cold water
8	eggs, separated
2	6-ounce cans frozen orange juice, defrosted
1	cup plus 3 tablespoons sugar, divided
1	cup heavy cream, chilled

Soften gelatin in cold water for 5 minutes. In a double boiler, beat egg yolks until thick and lemon colored. Add softened gelatin. Cook over simmering water, stirring constantly, until mixture lightly coats the spoon. Caution: Do not allow to boil. Remove from heat, stir in orange juice.

Transfer to a large mixing bowl and chill 30 minutes or until mixture thickens to a syrup. Whip cream until soft peaks form, beat in remaining sugar. Fold into orange mixture. Beat egg whites until frothy, gradually add 1 cup of sugar, continue beating until stiff peaks form. Fold into mousse.

Pour into a 1½ quart soufflé dish or other straight-sided dish which has had a lightly oiled collar of wax paper tied or taped around the outside, extending 2 or 3 inches above the rim. Smooth top with spatula, chill 4 hours or until firm. Remove collar and serve with Grand Marnier Sauce.

GRAND MARNIER SAUCE:

1	cup orange marmalade
2	tablespoons lemon juice
¼	to ½ cup Grand Marnier (to taste)
1½	to 2 tablespoons confectioners' sugar (to taste)
1	tablespoon cornstarch
¼	cup kirsch

Combine marmalade, lemon juice and Grand Marnier in a small saucepan. Mix sugar with cornstarch, add to marmalade mixture. Heat, stirring occasionally, until marmalade dissolves and mixture looks transparent. Place in a food processor or blender, purée. Cool, stir in kirsch, taste and adjust flavoring, chill.

8 servings

Apricot Mousse

1	6-ounce package dried apricots
1	12-ounce can apricot nectar
	Grated rind of 1 lemon
¼	cup apricot preserves
4	eggs, separated
¾	cup sugar
1	teaspoon cornstarch
1½	cups warm milk
1	tablespoon unflavored gelatin
½	cup warm water
1	cup heavy cream, whipped

Combine apricots, nectar and lemon rind in a saucepan, bring to a boil. Cover, reduce heat, simmer 30 minutes or until apricots are tender, add preserves. Place mixture in a food processor or blender, purée.

Beat egg yolks, sugar and cornstarch with an electric mixer until fluffy and lemon colored. Combine egg mixture and milk in a double boiler. Cook over simmering water, stirring constantly, until mixture coats the spoon.

Dissolve gelatin in warm water, stir into custard. Fold in apricot purée, chill until almost set (mixture will be firm around the edge, but not in center). Fold in whipped cream. Beat egg whites until firm, but not dry. Fold gently into mousse. Spoon into a 1½ quart souffle dish. Chill well before serving.

12 to 14 servings

Frozen Cappuccino in Demitasse

6	tablespoons Cappuccino mix (Italian-style instant coffee beverage)
6	tablespoons brandy, chilled
1	pint coffee ice cream, softened
⅓	cup crushed toffee candy bars
4	cinnamon sticks
	Whipped cream

Combine Cappuccino mix and brandy, stir until mix is dissolved. Fold in ice cream and candy. Spoon into demitasse cups, place in freezer. Just before serving, add cinnamon sticks and top with whipped cream.

4 servings

Fit for royalty!

Yogurt Mousse

4	teaspoons unflavored gelatin
¼	cup cold water
1½	cups heavy cream
½	cup sugar
2¼	cups plain yogurt
1	teaspoon vanilla extract

Soften gelatin in cold water for 10 minutes. Heat cream and sugar 5 minutes in a double boiler over simmering water, stirring constantly. Add gelatin, stir until dissolved. Transfer to a bowl, cool. Stir yogurt and vanilla into cream mixture.

Rinse a 1-quart mold with cold water, do not dry. Pour mixture into mold, cover with wax paper. Chill 2 hours or until firm. Unmold on serving dish.

6 to 8 servings

Refreshing with lightly sugared fresh berries or topped with Apricot, Grand Marnier or Strawberry-Raspberry Sauce.

Zucchini Chocolate Cake

A marvelous solution for a bountiful zucchini crop. This deserves equal billing with the ubiquitous carrot cake.

¾	cup butter, softened
2	cups sugar
3	eggs, at room temperature
2½	cups flour
2½	teaspoons baking powder
1½	teaspoons baking soda
1	teaspoon cinnamon
½	teaspoon salt
½	cup cocoa
2	teaspoons vanilla extract
½	cup buttermilk
2	cups grated peeled zucchini
1	cup chopped pecans

Preheat oven to 350°.

Grease 13 x 9-inch pan well.

Cream butter and sugar, add one egg at a time, beating well after each addition. Sift together flour, baking powder, baking soda, cinnamon and salt. Add to egg mixture. Stir in cocoa, vanilla and buttermilk, mix well. Fold in zucchini and pecans.

Pour batter into pan, bake 30 to 35 minutes or until cake tester inserted in center comes out clean. Garnish with whipped cream.

10 to 12 servings

Current River
Chocolate Sheet Cake

1	cup butter
½	cup cocoa
1	cup water
2	cups sugar
2	cups flour, unsifted
1	teaspoon baking soda
2	eggs, slightly beaten
½	cup sour cream or buttermilk
2	teaspoons vanilla extract

CHOCOLATE NUT ICING:

½	cup butter
¼	cup cocoa
6	tablespoons evaporated milk
1	16-ounce box confectioners' sugar
1	cup chopped nuts
1	teaspoon vanilla extract

Preheat oven to 350°.

Grease a 15½ x 10½-inch jelly roll pan well.

Combine butter, cocoa and water in a saucepan, bring to a full boil. While still hot, pour mixture over combined sugar, flour and baking soda, mix well. Add eggs, sour cream (buttermilk) and vanilla, mix well. Pour batter into pan, bake 15 minutes. Do not overbake. While cake is baking, make the icing. Ice cake immediately after removing from oven.

Mix butter, cocoa and milk in a saucepan, heat to boiling point. Add confectioners' sugar, nuts and vanilla, mix well. Additional milk may be added to make icing more spreadable.

20 to 24 servings

A sinfully rich and easy dessert. So named because it is always packed in the cooler for our annual spring float trip on the Current River.

Molded Chocolate Cake

¾	cup unsalted butter, softened
¾	cup sugar
8	eggs, separated
4	ounces semisweet chocolate
¼	cup strong coffee
3	tablespoons Amaretto, divided
3	tablespoons dark rum, divided
4	slices white bread (crusts removed), dried and torn into pieces
1	cup almonds, toasted and crushed, divided
	Pinch cream of tartar
½	cup chocolate syrup

Cream butter, gradually add sugar, mix well. Add 1 egg yolk at a time, beating well after each addition. Continue beating until light and fluffy.

Melt chocolate with coffee, add 2 tablespoons each Amaretto and rum, blend into egg-sugar mixture. Place bread in a food processor or blender, process into crumbs. Stir crumbs and ¾ cup almonds into chocolate mixture.

Beat egg whites with cream of tartar until stiff peaks form. Fold into chocolate mixture, pour into a well-greased 1½-quart pudding mold or bundt pan.

Cover cake tightly with mold cover or greased foil, place on rack in Dutch oven. Pour boiling water to within 1½ inches of top of mold, cover. Cook on burner over moderate heat for 1 hour.

Remove mold from water, dry carefully and uncover. Run a knife around the edge, invert on serving plate. Sprinkle with remaining almonds.

Mix remaining Amaretto and rum with syrup, heat. Drizzle sauce over cake.

8 servings

Lemon Sour Cream Pound Cake

½	cup butter
½	cup margarine
3	cups sugar
6	eggs
2	teaspoons lemon extract
3	cups flour, sifted with
½	teaspoon baking soda
1	cup sour cream

Preheat oven to 325°.

Beat butter and margarine with an electric mixer, gradually add sugar, mix until fluffy. Add eggs, one at a time, beating 1 minute on low or medium speed after each addition. Stir in lemon extract.

Sift in 1 cup of flour, stir in ½ cup of sour cream, mix; repeat, using remaining ingredients, ending with flour. Caution: Do not overbeat.

Transfer to a well-greased and lightly floured 10-inch tube or bundt pan. Place in lower portion of the oven. Bake 30 minutes, reduce heat to 300° and continue baking 45 minutes or until done. Cool in the pan 10 minutes, turn out on rack.

10 to 12 servings

The original contained a pound each of butter, sugar, flour and eggs. Regardless of its origin, pound cake is a delectable legacy, and my mother's recipe is a masterpiece from the standpoint of flavor and texture.

Cranberry Crunch

Tart and satisfying.

1	cup sugar
¾	cup water
2	cups fresh cranberries
5	apples
¼	cup lemon juice
1½	cups uncooked oatmeal
¾	cup packed brown sugar
½	cup butter, melted
1½	tablespoons flour

Preheat oven to 350°.

Mix sugar and water in a medium saucepan, bring to a boil over high heat, continue boiling 1 minute. Reduce heat. Add cranberries, cook until they pop, about 1 minute. Remove from heat.

Peel and core apples, slice thinly. Dip slices in lemon juice, place in greased 9-inch square baking dish. Pour cranberries over apples.

Combine oatmeal, brown sugar, butter and flour, mix well. Sprinkle over fruit. Bake 35 to 40 minutes or until topping is lightly browned.

9 servings

Blueberry Peach Cobbler

7	ripe peaches
1	pint blueberries
1	teaspoon grated lemon rind
1	tablespoon fresh lemon juice
⅛	teaspoon almond extract
¾	cup plus 5 tablespoons sugar
1	cup flour, sifted
1	teaspoon baking powder
½	teaspoon salt
1	egg, unbeaten
5	tablespoons butter, melted
1	teaspoon cinnamon
¼	teaspoon nutmeg

Preheat oven to 375°.

Coat a 9 x 13-inch baking dish with vegetable spray.

Blanch peaches, peel, cut in wedges. Spread peaches in dish, top with blueberries. Combine lemon rind, lemon juice, almond extract and 3 tablespoons sugar, sprinkle over fruit, set aside.

Sift together flour, ¾ cup sugar, baking powder and salt in a mixing bowl. Add egg, mix with fork until coarsely blended. Caution: Do not overblend. Sprinkle topping in a very thin layer over berries, leaving a few open areas. Drizzle butter over topping. Combine cinnamon, nutmeg and remaining sugar, sprinkle over topping.

Bake in top ⅓ of oven for 15 minutes. Increase temperature to 400°, bake 12 to 15 minutes until lightly browned. Allow to set for 20 minutes. Serve with sweetened Crème Fraîche.

Note: Unsweetened frozen fruit may be substituted; use a 20-ounce package of peaches and an 18-ounce package of blueberries. Defrost and drain before using.

10 to 12 servings

A summer symphony. Prepared with frozen fruit, this stellar dessert is a year-round favorite.

Ginger-Rum Pumpkin Pie

What a sensational conclusion to a traditional Turkey Day dinner!

3	eggs, separated
1½	cups solid pack pumpkin
½	cup packed dark brown sugar
¼	cup plus 2 tablespoons granulated sugar, divided
1	cup sour cream
¼	teaspoon salt
⅛	teaspoon nutmeg
2	ounces crystallized ginger, minced
3	tablespoons dark rum
1	9-inch pie shell, unbaked
1	cup heavy cream
	Slivered almonds, toasted

Preheat oven to 350°.

Beat egg yolks. Combine egg yolks, pumpkin, brown sugar, ¼ cup granulated sugar, sour cream, salt and nutmeg in a double boiler. Cook, stirring occasionally, over simmering water until mixture thickens, about 5 minutes. Remove from heat. Fold in ginger and rum, set aside.

Beat egg whites until foamy. Gradually beat in remaining sugar, continue beating until egg whites form stiff peaks. Fold into pumpkin mixture.

Turn into pie shell, bake 40 to 45 minutes until filling is set. Cool on rack.

Whip cream in a chilled mixing bowl until stiff. Cover pie with whipped cream, top with almonds.

6 to 8 servings

Kentucky High Day Pie

1	cup sugar
¼	cup cornstarch
2	eggs, beaten
½	cup butter, melted
¼	cup bourbon
1	cup chopped pecans
6	ounces semisweet chocolate chips
1	9-inch pie shell, unbaked

WHIPPED CREAM:

1	cup heavy cream, chilled, divided
1	tablespoon butter, softened
1	tablespoon sugar

Preheat oven to 350°.

Mix sugar and cornstarch, whisk into eggs. Add butter and bourbon, whisk after each addition. Stir in nuts and chocolate chips. Pour into crust, bake 45 to 50 minutes. Serve with Whipped Cream.

Blend 2 tablespoons cream with butter, add remaining cream. Whip to form soft peaks, gradually add sugar and whip until stiff.

8 servings

Growing up in Kentucky, I remember every Derby Day menu featured High Day Pie. This heavenly dessert is now a regular feature for legislative luncheons at the Mansion.

Blueberries with Lemon Mousse

5	eggs, separated
1	cup sugar, divided
	Juice of 2 large lemons
1	cup heavy cream, whipped
2	teaspoons grated lemon rind
1	quart blueberries

In a non-aluminum double boiler, beat egg yolks and ¾ cup of sugar until mixture becomes thick and lemon colored. Add lemon juice. Cook over simmering water, stirring constantly, until mixture heavily coats the spoon. Caution: Do not allow to boil. Remove from heat, cool.

Beat egg whites until stiff, fold into lemon mixture. Fold in whipped cream and lemon rind until mousse is smooth, chill.

Pour blueberries into a glass serving bowl, sprinkle with remaining sugar. Just before serving, cover blueberries with mousse.

8 servings

New England Baked Apples

2	tablespoons walnuts
6	firm tart apples
¼	cup lemon juice
¼	cup pure maple syrup
¼	cup water
1	tablespoon unsalted butter, melted

MAPLE CREAM SAUCE:

1¼	cups heavy cream
¼	cup pure maple syrup
¼	cup light corn syrup

Preheat oven to 350°.

Toast walnuts lightly in oven, chop fine. Core and pare upper third of each apple. Place in lightly-oiled baking dish, sprinkle with lemon juice. Combine syrup, water and butter, pour over apples.

Bake uncovered 30 minutes or until apples are tender, basting every 10 minutes. Place apples in dessert dishes, spoon on pan juices, sprinkle with walnuts. Serve with Maple Cream Sauce.

For sauce, combine cream, maple syrup and corn syrup in a saucepan. Reduce syrup mixture ⅓ by cooking over moderate heat about 10 minutes. Set pan in ice water, stir until cool, chill. Serve sauce cool, but not cold.

6 servings

Sophisticated version of an old-fashioned dessert.

Oranges in Wine

Excels in taste, appearance and ease of preparation. A perfect choice after a hearty main course or a Chinese stir-fry dinner.

¾	cup sugar
1	cup water
1	cup red port
2	whole cloves
	1-inch piece stick cinnamon
	1-inch piece vanilla bean, or ½ teaspoon vanilla extract
4	lemon slices
6	large seedless oranges
1	cup heavy cream, whipped and sweetened

Combine sugar and water in a saucepan, cook, stirring constantly, until sugar dissolves. Add port, cloves, cinnamon, vanilla and lemon slices. Bring to a boil, continue boiling for 15 minutes or until liquid becomes syrupy. Strain, discard flavorings, cool slightly.

While mixture boils, peel oranges, removing all the white membrane. Slice each orange thinly, keeping original shape. Place one sliced orange in each of 6 individual glass dessert dishes.

Pour warm syrup over oranges, refrigerate 4 hours or until thoroughly chilled. Top with whipped cream and garnish with a light sprinkle of grated orange zest.

6 servings

Peaches in Sherry Sabayon

6	large peaches, peeled and cut into thick wedges
	Juice of 1 lemon
	Grated rind of 1 lemon
4	egg yolks
1/3	cup sugar
3/4	cup cream sherry
	Toasted almonds, finely chopped

Place peaches in a bowl, sprinkle with lemon juice and rind. Chill 1 to 2 hours.

In a non-aluminum double boiler, beat egg yolks, sugar and sherry until thick and lemon colored. Cook over simmering water, stirring constantly, until mixture heavily coats the spoon. Caution: Do not allow to boil. Remove from heat, cool.

Drain peaches, discard lemon juice. Pour sherry sauce over peaches, chill. To serve, sprinkle almonds over sauce.

Note: Frozen unsweetened peaches may be substituted; defrost and drain well.

6 servings

The fresh peaches retain their lovely blush.

Poached Pears with Chocolate Sauce

To reduce preparation time or for those unexpected dinner guests, serve the chocolate sauce over canned unsweetened pear halves.

4	firm ripe pears
1	cup water
1	cup white port
¾	cup sugar
6	slices lemon
4	whole cloves
1	cinnamon stick
	1-inch piece vanilla bean or ½ teaspoon vanilla extract to taste
1	or 2 tablespoons calvados (to taste)
1	3-ounce package cream cheese, softened

Peel pears, cut in half lengthwise. Use a melon baller to remove cores. (To prevent pears from darkening, drop into a bowl of water containing a little lemon juice.)

In a non-aluminum saucepan, bring water, port, sugar, lemon, cloves, cinnamon stick and vanilla to a boil. Stir constantly until sugar dissolves, add drained pear halves. Reduce heat, simmer 30 minutes or until pears are tender, but not soft. Cool in syrup. Drain, chill pears, discard syrup.

Whip calvados into cream cheese, fill cavity of each pear. Arrange on serving plate cheese side down. To serve, drizzle Chocolate Sauce over each half.

CHOCOLATE SAUCE:

½	cup butter
2½	cups confectioners' sugar
⅔	cup evaporated milk
6	ounces unsweetened chocolate

Melt butter with sugar in a double boiler, add milk and chocolate. Cook uncovered 30 minutes over slightly boiling water. Caution: Do not stir. Remove from heat, beat. Serve warm.

Note: Add cream but not water for a thinner sauce. Two cups of sauce will be more than needed for the pears. The remaining sauce may be reheated in a double boiler or microwave for another use. It is excellent served over ice cream.

8 servings

Cappuccino Ice Cream

What could be a more perfect finale to an intimate dinner party than the combination of coffee and ice cream? A splash of coffee liqueur is a nice topping.

2¼	cups light cream
3	tablespoons instant coffee powder
12	egg yolks
1	cup plus 6 tablespoons sugar, divided
2	cups heavy cream
½	cup butter
2	teaspoons vanilla extract
2	tablespoons ground espresso coffee (not instant)

In a saucepan, slowly bring light cream and instant coffee to a boil. Remove from heat, cool. Place in refrigerator overnight, or chill in freezer briefly, but do not freeze.

Cream egg yolks and ½ cup plus tablespoons of sugar, set aside. In a 3½ to 4-quart saucepan, combine heavy cream and remaining sugar, stirring frequently, and slowly bring to a boil. Whisking constantly, add ⅓ of cream mixture to yolks. Pour this mixture back into saucepan, whisking constantly. Heat to just under boiling point. Remove from heat, quickly whisk in butter. Immediately place pan in a bowl of ice to stop cooking, stirring frequently until cool.

Pour through fine strainer. Beat in chilled coffee mixture and vanilla. Place in 6-quart ice cream maker, churn according to manufacturer's directions.

Transfer ice cream to large mixing bowl, add ground espresso, stir to mix. Scoop into a container and return to freezer.

2 quarts

Mocha Cocoa Torte

1½	cups crushed almond macaroons
½	gallon chocolate ice cream, softened
1½	cups chocolate syrup or fudge sauce, divided
½	gallon coffee ice cream, softened
¼	cup Irish Mist or Kahlua
½	cup crushed toffee candy bars

In a 10-inch spring-form pan, layer macaroons, chocolate ice cream and ½ cup chocolate syrup (fudge sauce), freeze. Add layer of coffee ice cream, pour on liqueur. Caution: Do not use more, it does not freeze. Top with candy. Freeze until firm, preferably overnight. Unmold on serving dish. Warm remaining syrup, serve with torte.

Note: Amaretto cookies may be substituted for macaroons.

12 servings

All my favorite things—almond macaroons, chocolate and toffee—in a frozen confection that's impossible to resist!

Lemon Sorbet

To refresh the palate during a multi-course dinner, or as a very light dessert following Chinese or Italian cuisine.

3	cups sugar
5	cups boiling water
1	tablespoon grated lemon rind
2	cups fresh lemon juice
2	tablespoons orange flower water
	Sugar (to taste)

Combine sugar and water, stirring unt sugar dissolves. Add lemon rind (yellow skin with no pith), juice and orang flower water. Pour into a shallow pa freeze. Using a food processor or a electric mixer, process until thick ar fluffy. Refreeze.

2 quarts

Cranberry Sorbet

Fashion a decorative orange "basket" for a fanciful presentation.

2	cups fresh whole cranberries
½	cup burgundy
1½	cups orange juice
1	cup sugar
1	teaspoon grated orange rind

Combine all ingredients in a saucepa stir over medium heat until cranberri are soft and break open. Pour mixtu through a fine strainer. Press cranberri through strainer with a wooden spoo discard pulp. Cool to room temperatur

Pour mixture into a 9 x 5-inch loaf pa Freeze until firm.

Spoon mixture into a food processor blender, process until light and fluff but do not let thaw. Refreeze.

Note: Frozen cranberries may be subs tuted; defrost and drain well befo using.

24 servings

Blueberry Kir Sauce

1	tablespoon butter
1	tablespoon cornstarch
¼	cup crème de cassis
¾	cup dry white wine
1	tablespoon lemon juice
1½	cups fresh blueberries
	Sugar (to taste)

Melt butter in a saucepan. Blend cornstarch and cassis until smooth, stir into butter. Add wine and lemon juice, cook, stirring constantly, until mixture is thick. Add blueberries, cook until blueberries begin to burst. Add sugar if desired. Cool and refrigerate.

5 servings

An adaptable dessert sauce. Try it over Yogurt Mousse, vanilla ice cream or lemon sherbet.

Caramel Nut Sauce

4	teaspoons butter
½	cup coarsely chopped pecans or slivered almonds
1	cup packed brown sugar
1	cup heavy cream

Melt butter in a small saucepan over medium-low heat, add nuts. Cook, stirring frequently, until nuts are lightly toasted. Add sugar and cream. Cook, stirring constantly, until sauce boils and sugar dissolves. Remove from heat, cool. Serve at room temperature over ice cream.

Variation: Caramel Nut-Chocolate Sauce—Add ¼ cup semisweet chocolate pieces to cooled sauce.

2 cups

We keep this on hand at the Mansion for those inevitable impromptu dinners.

Pecan Pie Cookies

A delectable addition to a holiday tea table.

1¼	cups butter, softened, divided
½	cup granulated sugar
½	cup plus 3 tablespoons dark corn syrup, divided
2	eggs, separated
2½	cups flour, unsifted
½	cup confectioners' sugar
½	cup chopped pecans

Cream 1 cup of butter and the granulated sugar on low speed with an electric mixer. Add ½ cup of corn syrup and egg yolks, beat until thoroughly blended. Gradually stir in flour. Chill dough several hours.

Refrigerate egg whites.

Combine confectioners' sugar, remaining butter and remaining corn syrup in a saucepan, mix well. Cook over medium heat, stirring occasionally, until mixture reaches a full boil. Remove from heat, stir in pecans, chill.

Preheat oven to 375°.

To make cookie fillings, shape ½ teaspoons of chilled pecan mixture into balls. Set aside, chill.

Slightly beat egg whites. Shape tablespoonfuls of dough into balls, brush very lightly with egg white. Place dough balls 2 inches apart on a greased cookie sheet, bake 5 minutes, remove from oven. Press filling balls into center of each cookie. Return to oven, bake 5 minutes or until lightly browned. Cool 5 minutes on cookie sheet, remove, cool completely on rack.

4 dozen

Butterscotch Refrigerator Cookies

1	6-ounce package butterscotch chips
½	cup butter, softened
⅔	cup packed light brown sugar
1	egg
1½	cups flour, sifted with
¾	teaspoon baking soda

Melt butterscotch chips over low heat, set aside. Cream butter, add sugar gradually until light and fluffy. Beat in egg and melted butterscotch chips. Add flour mixture to other ingredients, mix well. Shape into a 2-inch-in-diameter roll, wrap, chill overnight.

Preheat oven to 375°.

Cut in thin slices, bake 8 to 10 minutes on greased cookie sheets. Cool on rack.

4 dozen

A welcome treat in any child's school lunch box.

Mansion Brownies

5	ounces semisweet chocolate
⅔	cup butter
4	eggs
2	cups sugar
	Pinch of salt
1	cup flour
1	teaspoon baking powder
1	teaspoon vanilla extract
2	cups chopped pecans

Preheat oven to 325°.

Grease a 9 x 13-inch baking pan well.

Melt chocolate and butter in a saucepan. Beat eggs and sugar until fluffy, stir into chocolate mixture. Sift salt, flour and baking powder together, add to chocolate mixture with vanilla and pecans. Mix well.

Turn into pan, bake 40 minutes. Cool and cut.

2 dozen

A staple for our float trips, tailgates and informal suppers when dessert must be finger-food.

Peanut Butter Cup Cookies

1	15-ounce roll peanut butter cookie dough, from the dairy case
1	9-ounce package Reese's miniatures, paper wrappings removed

Preheat oven to 350°.

Cut well-chilled dough into 9 slices about 1 inch thick, quarter each slice. Drop quarter sections into well-greased miniature muffin tins. Bake 7 to 8 minutes or until puffy.

Remove from oven. Put 1 unwrapped peanut butter cup on each cookie. Bake 2 to 3 minutes until chocolate is soft. Loosen each cookie, let cool 5 minutes. Remove from tins, cool on rack.

36 cookies

Café Brûlot

1	lemon
1	orange
13	lumps sugar
5	whole cloves
2½	sticks cinnamon
¼	vanilla bean
1	cup cognac
4	to 6 cups strong hot coffee, freshly made

Peel lemon and orange, spiral fashion. (Reserve fruit for another use.)

Light fire under chafing dish.

Place lump sugar in chafing dish, add cloves, cinnamon, vanilla bean and peels.

Warm cognac in a ladle, ignite. Very slowly ladle cognac into chafing dish. Caution: Be careful not to extinguish flame. While still flaming, pour in hot coffee. Serve immediately in demitasse cups.

10 servings

Following a state dinner when guests are happily replete, Café Brûlot is often served in the Library or from the Steinway piano in the Double Parlor.

ACCOMPANIMENTS

Easy Cheese Soufflé

4	eggs, lightly beaten
1	cup heavy cream
¾	cup grated cheddar cheese
¾	cup grated Parmesan cheese
⅔	teaspoon salt
	Freshly ground pepper to taste

Preheat oven to 450°.

Combine eggs, cream, cheeses, salt and pepper, mix well. Pour into buttered individual ramekins or a 1-quart soufflé dish, fill container ⅔ full. Bake 15 minutes in ramekins, 25 minutes in soufflé dish, until golden and puffy. Soufflé is done when knife inserted between center and side comes out clean.

4 servings

Amazingly simple to prepare and simply delicious.

Kentucky Cheese Grits

3	eggs, well beaten
½	cup milk
¾	cup butter, melted
1	teaspoon salt, or to taste
1	teaspoon paprika
	Dash of Tabasco
½	pound cheddar cheese, grated
½	pound garlic cheese, sliced
1½	cups uncooked grits

Preheat oven to 350°.

In a double boiler, combine ingredients, except grits, in order given, mix well. Warm slowly, stirring constantly, until cheese melts. Meanwhile, cook grits according to package directions. Combine warm grits and warm cheese mixture. Taste and adjust seasoning.

Turn into greased 9 x 13-inch baking dish, bake uncovered 45 minutes.

8 to 10 servings

A sorority sister from the University of Kentucky gave this recipe to me years ago. Since, it has become a mainstay of brunch menus, often served with Glazed Canadian Bacon, Eggs Florentine and platters of fresh fruit with Poppy Seed Dressing.

Brown Rice and Pine Nut Casserole

The taste is as superb as the aroma. Excellent served as an accompaniment to Dove in Wine or Lamb Shanks with Chutney. A salad of seasonal greens provides color and crunch.

½	cup pine nuts
¼	cup butter, divided
1	cup uncooked brown rice
½	cup bulgur
1	large onion, chopped
1	cup minced fresh parsley, divided
6	tablespoons finely minced fresh chives or scallions
¼	teaspoon salt
¼	teaspoon pepper
3	14-ounce cans beef or chicken broth

Preheat oven to 375°.

Sauté pine nuts in 2 tablespoons of butter over moderate heat for 5 minutes until brown, stirring occasionally. Add remaining butter, rice, bulgur and onion. Sauté 10 minutes, stirring frequently. Transfer to a buttered 2-quart casserole. Combine ¾ cup of parsley with chives (scallions), salt and pepper; stir into casserole. Bring broth to a boil; stir into rice mixture.

Bake uncovered 1 hour and 15 minutes or until done. Before serving, sprinkle with remaining parsley.

8 servings

Rice and Mushroom Casserole

2	cups sliced onions
2	cups sliced fresh mushrooms
½	cup butter
1	cup beef consommé
1	cup water
1	cup uncooked rice
	Salt and freshly ground pepper to taste

Preheat oven to 350°.

Sauté onions and mushrooms in butter, add consommé and water. Add rice, mix well, season with salt and pepper. Taste and adjust seasoning. Transfer to a buttered 2-quart casserole, bake covered 45 minutes or until done. Garnish with snipped chives.

6 servings

A family favorite that appears frequently on the Mansion buffet table. The dish may be assembled in advance and baked just prior to serving.

Orange Rice

¼	cup butter, melted
1	cup uncooked long-grain rice
½	teaspoon salt
2	cups chicken broth
½	cup dry white wine
	Juice of 1 orange
	Grated rind of 1 orange
	Salt and freshly ground pepper to taste
	Chopped Italian parsley

Preheat oven to 350°.

Place butter, rice, salt, broth and wine in buttered 2-quart casserole, stir well. Cover, bake 45 minutes until feathery. Add orange juice and rind, season with salt and pepper. Return to oven, bake 10 minutes. Taste and adjust seasoning, toss well. Sprinkle with parsley.

8 servings

Coveted in the Far East as the staff of life, rice is as nourishing as it is versatile. The orange and wine flavors particularly complement roasted chicken, duck or goose.

Crêpes

No freezer should be without a supply of both entrée and dessert crêpes.

⅔	cup milk
⅔	cup water
1	cup flour
3	eggs
¼	teaspoon salt
3	tablespoons butter, melted

Gradually whisk milk and water into flour until smooth, whisk in eggs, salt and butter. Heat a non-stick 6- to 7-inch crêpe pan until drops of water jump and sputter on surface, brush lightly with butter.

Pour 2 tablespoons batter into center of pan, quickly rotate pan so batter evenly coats the bottom. Cook 30 seconds or until bottom of crêpe is brown. Turn and cook briefly (turned side will not brown as well). Batter may be thinned with a few drops of milk. Cool, stack with wax paper between each crêpe. Store in refrigerator for 2 to 3 days or freeze.

Dessert crêpes: Decrease liquids to ½ cup measurements, eggs to 2, and add 2 egg yolks, ¼ cup orange juice and ¼ cup sugar. Other ingredients remain the same. Follow directions above for dry and liquid ingredients.

20 crêpes

Yorkshire Pudding

2	eggs
1	cup milk
1	tablespoon water
1	cup flour*
¼	teaspoon salt
¼	cup beef drippings

Preheat oven to 450°.

Combine eggs, milk and water. Beat well. Stir in flour* (use ½ cup for a very delicate pudding) and salt. Mix until evenly blended, but do not over-mix. Refrigerate at least 30 minutes before baking.

Heat a 9-inch square ovenproof pan or 9-inch pie pan containing the beef drippings. Beat egg mixture again and pour into prepared pan. Bake until puffed and brown, about 30 minutes. Cut into squares or wedges and serve immediately. (Pudding does fall.)

Note: Serve with Standing Rib Roast. Unless the roast has plenty of fat, add extra suet to the roasting pan so there will be plenty for the pudding.

4 to 6 servings

A classic with roast beef, Yorkshire pudding is often substituted for the usual starch. The pan drippings must be sizzling hot or the pudding won't puff.

Cranberry-Apple-Pear Sauce

A must with the Thanksgiving turkey! Served with warmed Brie and lahvosh, this is a festive, colorful addition to a holiday table.

2	pounds fresh cranberries
4	apples, pared, cored and diced
3	pears, pared, cored and diced
2	cups golden raisins
2	cups sugar
1	cup fresh orange juice
2½	tablespoons grated orange rind
2	teaspoons cinnamon
¼	teaspoon freshly grated nutmeg
½	cup plus 2 tablespoons orange-flavored liqueur

Place all ingredients, except liqueur, in a large saucepan. Bring to a boil, reduce heat. Simmer uncovered 45 minutes, stirring frequently until mixture thickens. Remove from heat, stir in liqueur, cool. Refrigerate at least 4 hours. Serve sauce slightly chilled with pork, chicken or turkey.

6 cups

Tomato Chutney

Wonderful for gift-giving and a treasure on your own pantry shelf. Home-grown tomatoes are essential.

7	pounds ripe tomatoes, quartered
3	pounds sugar
1	pint cider vinegar
12	to 16 sticks cinnamon (to taste)
2	tablespoons whole cloves

Combine all ingredients in a large non-aluminum pan. Simmer 6 to 8 hours, stirring every 2 hours. Spoon into sterilized pint jars.

3 to 3½ pints

Horseradish Mousse

1	tablespoon unflavored gelatin
¼	cup cold water
2	cups low-calorie cottage cheese
1	tablespoon grated onion
3	tablespoons prepared horseradish
¼	cup skim milk
	Few drops of Tabasco sauce
	Salt and freshly ground pepper to taste

Soften gelatin in water. Combine cheese, onion and horseradish in a food processor or blender, process until smooth.

Heat milk in a small saucepan, add gelatin, stir over low heat until dissolved. Add to cheese mixture. Stir in Tabasco, season with salt and pepper. Spoon into a lightly-oiled 1-pint mold, refrigerate. Unmold and serve with barbecued brisket.

2 cups

This piquant mousse adds a touch of refinement to barbecued brisket or chicken. Attractive garnished with a selection of pickles and olives.

Mustard Dill Sauce

⅔	cup Dijon mustard
¼	cup sugar
¼	cup white wine vinegar
	Salt and freshly ground pepper to taste
¼	cup sour cream
⅔	cup vegetable oil
⅔	cup chopped fresh dill

Combine all ingredients, except oil and dill, in a food processor or blender, process until smooth. With machine running, pour oil in a thin stream until thoroughly incorporated. If added too fast, sauce may separate. Add dill, mix, using an on-and-off technique, until blended. Taste and adjust seasoning, refrigerate. Sauce will keep 2 weeks.

2 cups

A zestful addition to beef, salmon or steamed vegetables.

Cucumber Dill Sauce

Guaranteed to excite your taste buds. Developed to accompany Kit's Poached Salmon on the Grill, it is equally good with fresh trout or white bass.

⅔	cup unsweetened Crème Fraîche (see index)
1	large cucumber, peeled, seeded and cut into pieces
⅔	cup mayonnaise
⅔	cup sour cream
2	tablespoons fresh lemon juice
¼	cup packed chopped fresh dill*
	Cracked salt and freshly ground white pepper to taste
	Cayenne pepper to taste

Make Crème Fraîche at least 2 to 3 days before preparing this sauce.

Finely chop cucumber in a food processor or blender. Place in a colander, sprinkle lightly with salt. Let drain at least 30 minutes, pressing out liquid, set aside. (One cucumber should yield the packed ¼ cup required.)

Whisk together Crème Fraîche, mayonnaise and sour cream. Add cucumber, lemon juice and dill. Season with salt, pepper and cayenne pepper, blend well. Taste and adjust seasoning. Refrigerate until ready to use.

Note: Sauce may be thinned with a little white wine or lemon juice. If lemon juice is used, be careful that sauce is not too tart.

*Fresh dill is imperative in this recipe.

2½ cups

Horseradish Garlic Sauce

2	egg yolks
1	tablespoon white wine vinegar
½	teaspoon salt
1	teaspoon sugar
¼	teaspoon white pepper
⅔	cup peanut oil
⅓	cup vegetable oil
3	tablespoons prepared horseradish, or to taste
3	fresh garlic cloves, minced, or to taste

Place yolks, vinegar, salt, sugar and pepper in a food processor or blender, mix lightly. With machine running, combine oils and add in a thin stream until thoroughly incorporated. If added too fast, sauce may separate.

Add ½ of the horseradish and ½ of the garlic, taste before adding remainder. Chill before serving. Garnish with snipped chives or sprigs of fresh parsley.

Note: Sauce may be prepared one week ahead.

1¼ cups

A southern European sauce at home in Missouri. Equally delicious with cold meats, seafood and vegetables.

Béarnaise Sauce

¼	cup wine vinegar
¼	cup dry white wine
1	tablespoon minced shallots
1	tablespoon minced fresh tarragon or ½ tablespoon dried tarragon
	Salt and freshly ground pepper to taste
½	cup butter
3	egg yolks
½	tablespoon lemon juice
1½	tablespoons water

Combine vinegar, wine, shallots, tarragon, pinch of salt and ⅛ teaspoon of pepper in a small saucepan. Cook over medium heat until liquid is reduced to 2 tablespoons. Pour mixture into a sieve, press to extract all liquid. Reserve liquid, discard mixture.

Melt butter over low heat. Combine egg yolks, ¼ teaspoon salt, pepper, lemon juice and water in a food processor or blender, process 90 seconds. Bring butter to a boil. With machine running, add butter (do not use milky residue) in a thin stream until thoroughly incorporated. If added too fast, sauce may separate. Sauce should thicken to the consistency of mayonnaise.

Add reserved 2 tablespoons of liquid, blend, using an on-and-off technique. Taste and adjust seasoning. Serve warm. If not used immediately, turn into bowl and set bowl in a pan of tepid water.

1 cup

Crème Fraîche

4	cups heavy cream
1	tablespoon buttermilk
	Confectioners' sugar

Combine cream and buttermilk in a large jar, cover. Store in a warm place away from drafts for 24 to 36 hours until thick. In a warm kitchen, crème will be ready in 24 hours. Crème keeps 2 to 3 weeks refrigerated in a tightly sealed jar. Add sugar to taste.

4 cups

A large jar of this homemade version of French cream can always be found in the Mansion refrigerator. Unlike commercial sour cream, Crème Fraîche will not curdle in a hot sauce. Sugared Crème Fraîche is a delicious topping for apple pie, fresh fruit or Blueberry Peach Cobbler.

MISSOURI MANSION PRESERVATION, INC. BOARD OF DIRECTOR

Honorary Members	Mrs. John M. Dalton
	Governor and Mrs. Warren E. Hearnes
	Mrs. Guy B. Park
	Mrs. Lloyd C. Stark
	Governor and Mrs. Joseph P. Teasdale
Restoration Architect	Theodore J. Wofford, A.I.A.
	Murphy, Downey, Wofford &
	Richman/Architects, Inc.
MMPI Executive Director	Mary Patricia Herlihy Abele
MMPI Secretary	Deborah Bowers Koerner

STATE OF MISSOURI, OFFICE OF ADMINISTRATION

Division of Design and Construction Director	Walter H. Johnson
Architect, Project Manager	Robert E. Lee
Governor's Mansion Staff Mansion Assistant	Lois Glasscock May
Social Secretary	Kathryn Gardner Fisher
Mansion Cook	Norma Trask Carr
Mansion Housekeeper	Harriett Tichelkamp Ortmeyer

Editor-in-Chief	*Carolyn Reid Bond*
Editor	*June Jamieson Hughes*
Historical Text	*Conger Beasley, Jr.*
Recipe Editor	*Sandy James Coldsnow*
Design	*Kroh/Hunter Design* *Mary Lou Kroh* *Annemarie Hunter*
Restoration Architect	*Theodore J. Wofford, A.I.A.*
Official Photographers	*Hugo H. Harper* *Neil W. Sauer*
Project Coordinator	*Mary Patricia Herlihy Abele*

Project Co-Chairmen	*Mary Shaw Branton*
	Marilyn Tweedie Shutz
Project Advisor	*Karen Winfrey Craft*
State Recipe Testing Chairman	*Courtney Risner Earnest*
State Recipe Coordinator	*Susan Trainor Price*
State Marketing Chairman	*Linda Hickerson Cozad*
Area Marketing Chairmen	
Jefferson City	*Wilmoth Mason Hendren*
Kansas City	*Linda Hickerson Cozad*
St. Louis	*Marjorie Kalb McCown*
Out-State Missouri	*Susan Trainor Price*
Distribution Chairman	*Dorothy Atwood Nash*

Photographs   *Hugo H. Harper and Neil W. Sauer, iv, 43, 46, 56, 61, 62, 63,*
64, 129, 130-131, 132, 181, 182, 183, 184
George Laur, 11
Leonard Lujan and Victor Hasselblad, Inc. Cameras, i
Gary Sutton, iii
Missouri Department of Natural Resources, 14
Missouri Mansion Preservation, Inc. Archives, 4, 31, 32, 34, 36,
37, 38, 39, 40, 41, 48, 49, 50, 51, 52, 53, 57, 60, 65
The St. Louis Art Museum, 21
The St. Louis Mercantile Library Association, 10
State Historical Society of Missouri, 12, 13, 16, 28, 30, 33

Illustrations   *All design motifs illustrated in PAST & REPAST are taken from
stenciling and wallpaper patterns of the restored Executive Man-
sion.*

Flower Arrangements   *Lois Glasscock May, Mansion Assistant*
Barbara Forrester Rahm, Artistic Consultant
H. Rex Forsyth, Designer

Missouri Mansion Preservation, Inc. gratefully acknowledges the following people
for their contributions to the success of *PAST & REPAST* and regrets that a
printer's deadline prohibits a compete listing of volunteers participating in this
project:

Kathryn Gardner Fisher, Kathy Ramsay Foulke, Kristana Michelle Harper, Alber-
ta Plummer Holcomb, Deborah Bowers Koerner, Phyllis Fox Kraft, Lois Glasscock
May, Douglas G. Petty, Neil Christopher Sauer, Jr., Betsey Transou Solberg, Sally
Biles Sprague, Marie Larson Tompkins, Mariann Hopson Tow, Linda Brown
Urben, Leslie Marguerite Westbrook, Bonnie Winston and everyone who has
contributed time and talents to the project.

236

Area Recipe Testing Chairmen

Bethany
Helen Israel
Bolivar
Carol Robertson Roberts
Boonville
Joyce Gowan Abele
Butler
Mary Braschler Arnold
Camdenton
Claudia Barbee Parrish
Cape Girardeau
Mary Hunter Kinder
Chillicothe
Lou Skelton Cowherd
Clinton
Sue Stewart Cochran
Columbia
Judy Haynie Culley
Crocker
Norma Lea Anderson Mihalevich
Dexter
Pam Rodgers Kruse
Eldon
Maxine Anderson Bond*
Lucille Turner*
Fayette
Kitty Kaufman Greiner
Festus
Betty McKee Govero
Fulton
Martha Beck Morgan
Grandview/Lee's Summit
Mary Ann McCornack Ewert
Greenfield
Jane Robinson Preston
Hannibal
Nicky Price Clayton
Hartville
Wilda Hunter Cogdill
Herculaneum
Sherry Rosenberg Gielow
Hermann
Carol Rohlfing Kallmeyer
Higginsville
Tillie Stumpenhaus Erdman

Independence
Beverly Hull Constance
Jefferson City
Barbara Nice Brownlee
Joplin
Barbara Pearson Green
Jonesburg
Lillian Lagemann Sutor
Kansas City
Carol Burns Bayer
Sara Shipp Hoecker
JoAnn Hughes Sullivan
Kennett
Judy Gosney Haggard
Kimberling City
Betty Pearson Connell
Kirksville
Marie Frew Laughlin*
Leslie Wood White*
Liberty
Judith Fulkerson Ferguson
Linn
Linda Turner Maassen
Louisiana
Lucy Convy Sheppard
Marshall
Donna Klepper Huston*
Laurie Spreen Short*
Marshfield
Phyllis Marlin Fraker
Mexico
Alice Lehne Leonatti
Moberly
Carolyn Canon Koffman
Monett
Nancy Weems Clapper
Neosho
Bonnie Douglass Douglas
Owensville
Geraldine Ruffner Price
Paris
Lucille Fisher Blades
Perryville
Marilyn Stapleton Kiefner
Poplar Bluff
Jeannette Frost Harrell

Portageville
Shelly Clayton Fisher
Richmond
Valerie Kistler Miller
Rolla
Ellen Ogle O'Donnell
Rothville
Lorene Kelley Carpenter
St. Joseph
Shirley Mahaffey McCord
St. Louis
Kathy Rule Beilein
Marion Bischoff Black
Marjorie Kalb McCown
Jacqueline Thaman Niekamp*
Patricia Kligman Steinbach
Mary Jane Stock Thaman*
Salem
Beulah Hanning Chafin
Sedalia
Janet Hartin Monsees
Sikeston
Anne Burgess Rowe
Springfield
Martha Dean McLean*
Mary Guidry Williams*
Martha Stanley Wright*
Steele
Frances Womack Haggard
Union
Charlotte Webster Richman
Warsaw
Marilyn Roark Drake
West Plains
Billie Kay Farrar Gohn

*Co-Chairmen

Recipe Testers

Mary Patricia Herlihy Abele
Jan Litton Abset
Juanita Montgomery Adams
Mary Robertson Adams
Jan Gampper Ager
Elizabeth Crawford Alberts
Mildred Powers Alder
Ronnie Kreh Alewel
Thelma Michaud Alexander
Wilma Towe Alexopoulos
Harriet Snow Allen
Jane Collins Allen
Neva Dell Gemeinhardt Anderson
Jeanne Kaufman Ansehl
Sharon Duff Arbanas
Bunny Armstrong
Claire Byrne Arnold
Myrtis Riley Arp
James Atchison
Charlotte Atchison
Elizabeth Berry Atkins
Luella Hardy Attebery
Judy Letcher Aufdenburg
Erma Eskra Auxter
Elmira Evans Baiotto
Sally Aton Baird
Glenda Friar Baker
Margaret Kirk Baldwin
LaVeda Ferguson Banken
Becky Sisler Barbour
Pamela Kirkendoll Barkley
Emily Keyes Barksdale
Elizabeth Mitchell Barlow
Ida Beem Barnes
Ann Liggett Bates
Nora Kelly Bauman
Edzard Baumann
Bickley Hillyard Bayer
Mary Beard
Kay Bumgarner Beck
Colette Winn Becke
Mary Tracy Beckette
Ethel Autry Beechwood
Edna Burl Beissenherz
Marilyn Weber Bell
Marise Steele Benson
Patricia Springgate Berlin
Beatrice Peterson Berry
Gene Singleton Beynon
Neva Beals Bishop
Carol Culver Bitting
Cynthia Nangle Bitting
Marcelene Carlile Black
Vad Dickerson Black
Nancy Browning Blackwell
Linda Vanlandingham Blades
Jean Tucker Blalock
Suzanne Chubbuck Bland
Frances Wallace Blankenship

Kathleen Connell Blevins
Vicki Blevins
Imogene Smallwood Boeger
Kim Bohl
Doris Pickens Bohon
Mildred Tucker Bohon
Phyllis Aufderheide Boillot
Nancy Bland Boise
Janet Boisseau
Betty Booker
Sally Elliott Borello
Madeline Allen Boucher
Mabel Snyder Bower
Carol Kreisel Bowling
Betty Woodrow Bowman
Sharon McKee Boyer
Mary Jane Boylson
Mary Lou Nance Brace
Doris Martin Bradley
Shirley Wyeth Bradley
Vickie Anderson Bradley
Eric Brandt
Vickie Stephens Brandt
Ruth Lovercamp Bredehoeft
Ann Drake Breshears
Nancy Bridwell
Patricia Avis Brison
Alvina Britz
Gestle Swinea Brockett
Grace Rosenthal Brod
Jonelle Baker Brown
Alice Rowley Brownlee
Jane Egender Bruening
Lou Pollock Brydon
Veronica Meyer Buber
Marilyn Wilson Bueker
Barbara Ehart Burch
Joan Burns
Janet Heckel Burruss
Emma Strawther Byrd
Marlene Deaver Cable
Mary Jo Meyer Cable
Karen Taylor Cagle
Susan Schien Callis
Camdenton High School World
  Foods Class
Felice Lieberman Campbell
Joanne Ballinger Cannon
Dorothy Hammond Carlson
Ernestine Baxler Carroll
Cathy Carter
Naomi Davis Carter
Saundra Dodge Carter
Medah Stewart Cash
Edna Evsby Cason
Roswitha Wagner Caudle
Nancy Hotz Caverly
Georgia Mae Chapman
Nan Nichols Chapman

Mary Childers
Dede Sheldon Childress
Penny Hawkins Childress
Pat Chmela
Pat Murphy Ciersdorff
Lori Clapper
Loretta Wilkinson Clark
Katherine Hawkins Clarke
Bernadette Castle Cleary
Ann Whittier Closser
Velma Koenke Coate
Mary Harned Codding
Nancy Coffey
Dorothy Boldin Cohen
Helen Murphy Cohrs
Betty Willert Coil
Sandy James Coldsnow
Shirley Garrison Coleman
Helen Sperry Collins
Eky Brown Combs
Patti Thomas Connell
Deborah Bucher Cooper
Anne Miller Copeland
Frances Armstrong Corcoran
Clare Curran Coulter
Mary Wickham Coutts
Kathryn Cullen Cox
Patricia Patterson Cox
Karen Winfrey Craft
Dorothy Noel Crank
Marijo Jarboe Crawford
Carolyn Eichhorn Crews
Gretchen Fink Crossett
Arvilla Hughes Crouch
Carol Sewald Cunningham
Ula Senee Curtis
Mary Grace Kemoll
  Cusumano
Dana Hawkins Dallmeyer
Marianne Haggard Dalton
Berna Fondren Daugherty
Patti Patten Davidmeyer
Jean Bohrer Davidson
Mary Anne Yasskee Davidson
Ann Connell Davis
Charlene Giehrke Davis
Frances Baldwin Davis
Alberta James Daw
Marie Pizzo Dawson
Sue DeBoer
Gloria Ellis Deems
Joyce Greiner Dement
Fran Fore Dennison
Ann King Dickinson
Alberta Tibbits Dickman
Rosemary Schmitt Dieckhaus
Joan Dixon Dietzman
Nita Moore Dison
Martha Turk Dodson

Val Donnell
Jody Willmann Dorr
Thelma Breshears Douglas
Linda Huckett Dowdy
Lynda Crockett Dowdy
Jo Barrett Drum
Barbara Benne Dudley
Inez Windmeyer Duncan
Margaret Rutz Duncan
Leoda Morris Dunton
Dorothy Lane Dustman
Courtney Risner Earnest
Beverly Schowalter Easter
Ruth Poe Eastman
Marilyn Stratman Eckelkamp
Mary Elizabeth Edgington
Mary Lee Crowder Edgington
Julie Eggleston
Patricia Hull Eisler
Brunita Hedrick England
Marjon Malmo Ensminger
Patricia Smith Erker
Rook Sprouse Evans
Nikki Norman Fahnestock
Anne Graff Fairchild
Mary Gerling Farris
Elaine Fassold
Jane Hougen Fast
Suellyn Thomas Felker
Helen Carroll Finch
Carolyn Mueller Fischer
Ester Witteg Fisher
Rosemarie Grabbe Fisher
Cynthia Wania Flach
Elynor Keyser Flegel
Art Fleming
Becky Weaver Fleming
Mary Louise Maddox Fleming
Sheila Lanson Flom
Carolyn Ford
Hannah Bartlett Ford
Martha Knott Fowlkes
Helen Dyche Fraker
Jackie Cox Fraker
Marsha Cunningham Fraker
Susan Ketteman Franano
Ruth Fuerst Francka
Mary Ann Barker Frazee
Martha Reid Fredd
Joanne Frederick
Carolyn Bowles Frick
Susan Harkey Frogge
Kathryn Green Froman
Ann Yeager Frost
Karen Endburgh Fry
Mytle Fleshman Fuenfhausen
Carolyn Jenkins Fulkerson
Karla Knapp Gann
Margery Noyes Gantt

Kay Yadon Garrett
Fran McClure Gathmann
Lucile Simmons Geary
Karen Schilling Gibbs
Betty Bean Gifford
Jane Preble Gillan
Liz Gahlberg Gladney
Nancee Parsons Glaser
Judy Levine Glassman
George Gleason
Dorothy Savana Glover
Shirley Carnahan Gooch
Margaret Peden Goode
Janet Murray Goodwin
Janet Haynie Gordon
Patti Wolf Gould
Marlese Lowe Gourley
Alicia Kline Govero
Brenda Bartlett Graves
Jeanne Yaeger Grebe
Marjorie Greer Greene
Kay Richardson Greer
Robin Brown Greger
Sue Hyslop Grobe
Kassie Gerber Grossman
Marjorie Weldon Hahn
Jane Price Hall
Connie Gamlin Halstead
Elaine Rainey Hamburg
Judy Coleman Hancock
Melissa Haney
Dorothy Selby Harp
Rose Mary Jennings Harris
Jan Maerz Harrison
Thomas Harte
Jane Wyrick Hartley
Louise Lueke Hauck
Janet Keith Hawkins
Virginia Hammer Hawley
Frances Baker Hays
Libby Sealan Heineneann
Audrey Noring Heins
Dorothy Williams Helde
Jessie Giles Henderson
Annabel Samuelson Hendrich
Kelly Saunders Hendrich
Cindy Swanson Hendricks
Joyce Layton Hennemann
Nancy LaFevers Henry
Raona Miller Hentz
Betty Shull Hertzog
Joan Herx
Nettie Freeman Heyle
Rochelle Albert Hicks
Sally Woolwine Higgins
Pat Flynn Hilkemeyer
Lesli Simmons Hill
Mabel Montgomery Hill
Sybil Hill

Rosemary Huxol Hirschl
Karl Hirter
Leta Tucker Hodge
Carolyn Hoefer Hogan
Linda Long Holland
Gisela Hamann Horr
Carol Fishman Housh
Patricia Houts
Fern Stephens Huff
Jane Van Dyke Huff
Marion Pearl Huffman
Mildred Price Huffman
Caye Bugg Hughes
Cookie Bernardel Hunley
Virginia Parks Hupp
Barbara Wilcoxson Icenogle
Judith Kleinschmidt Iffrig
Dorothy Callaway Isdell
Carole Jones Isley
Gladys Doyle Israel
JoAnn Whiteside Jackson
Susan Thompson Jackson
Wanda Wilkerson Jackson
Lourine Rhoades James
Marietta Jonas Jayne
Anita Schooling Jean
Cissie Mayer Jenkins
Eola Terry Johnson
Helen Pitkin Johnson
Marty Walker Johnson
Sonya Welch Johnson
Valera Green Johnson
Deanne Pauley Jones
Pat Thomas Jones
Suzanne Chapman Jones
Quarrier Bloch Jones
Sandra Henderson Joplin
Ruby Joseph
Shirley Peterson Juliff
Chelsea Stanley Kehde
Stephanie Maehr Keith
Nadine Sloas Kelley
Mary Ramsay Kelley
Elaine Johnson Kent
Carol Judy Kent
Sylvia Smith Kesler
Wilma Weinkein Kiefer
Patricia Barton Kiefner
Betty Black Killingsworth
Charlotte Proett King
Ellen Hancock King
Wylma Bayless Kiser
Mary Ann Crede Klebba
Maria Matiasovska Klestinec
Sharon Larson Knapp
Elizabeth Ann Knote
Pat Binder Koenigsfeld
Deborah Bowers Koerner
Hazel Roberts Kohring

Chris Elman Kottmeier
Chris Remke Krautmann
Mary Ann Reynolds Krey
Barbara Vander Heyden Kruse
Elene Dubman Kweskin
Therese Chamberlain Lachmund
Sherry Cromwell Lacy
Janet Palsa Land
Marion Miller Lankford
Marguerite Buzzard Lawson
Cynthia Ahlbrandt Ledbetter
Sharon Roberson Lehar
Margery Troppman Lehenbauer
Mary Mansfield Lehne
Beth Noel Leicht
Juanita Leick
Sue Lemons
Joan Sawyer Lewis
Kristin Lewis
Helen Hosford Lindsey
Anita Bean Link
Catherine Weller Link
Celeste Chambers Lipscomb
Linda Wiechert Littleton
Karen Saint-Erne Loeffelholz
Susan Hoppe Logie
Alberta Barnstorff Logue
Janice Klaus Loman
Judith Campbell Long
Jennifer Lowe
Sherry Lowery
Janet Allen Luchfield
Jeana Gunn Lukowski
Ann MacCarthy
Talbot Leland MacCarthy
Marie Falk McClard
Mabel Poe McCormick
Dottie Burgess McCoy
Mary Brockett McCulloch
Susan Schell McCullough
Mariola Pauley McCuskey
Maureen Durkin McDonnell
Nancy Scarborough McElyea
Jaye Eddie McGuire
Dorothy Gleason McIntosh
Faye Samuels McIntosh
Jean Carter McIntosh
Carol Brown McKay
Mary Harrison McKinny
Darla Blevins Macoubrie
Carolyn Slayton Mainey
Narene Owens Mangrum
Anne Farr Manion
Fern Ferrier Manley
Laddie Martin Mann
Cathy Evans Marshall
Charolyn Brown Martin
Jan Wilson Martinette
Martha Dent Mason

Henrietta Hendrich Massie
Vicki Zuber Massman
Marie Mathieson
Lois Glasscock May
Ann Marshall Medlock
Helen Lawyer Melone
Betty Beck Mengel
Eva Dickerson Mercier
Marlene Mieser Meyer
Bernice Thaman Mezera
Elvira Baum Migliazzo
Janice Pace Miller
Laurie Wolf Miller
Marjorie Groves Mills
Sally Minor
Barbara Henderson Mitchell
Martha Powell Mitchell
Mildred Booth Mitchell
Shirley Sharp Mitchell
Sharon Preston Mlika
Elizabeth Sexton Mobley
Ruby Bremer Monsees
Judy Harris Moore
Linda Blades Moots
Willie Buckner Morgan
Jean McMillan Morris
Jean Melton Mowrer
Dorothy Heathman Mullendore
Barbara Lankford Mullin
Janet Johnson Murray
Helen Brown Mutti
Kaylynne Mekemson Myers
Elizabeth Littleton Myracle
Peggy Jennings Nail
Dorothy Atwood Nash
Rose Marie Danz Neher
Ellyn Fine Neise
Ruth Nixon Nethery
Barbara Bomford Newman
Ruth Patton Nichols
Verona Schmidt Nichols
Sherry Kennedy Nielsen
Theresa Speaks Nims
Annalee Bernstein Nissenholtz
Beverly Homra Noffel
Pamela Mathews Norris
Thelma Smith Norris
Daniel Smith Norton
Shirley Gennari Nottebrok
Mary Roudebush Nowotny
Ruth Zirkle Oberhelman
Rebecca Culpepper O'Connor
Julie Ann O'Donnell
Mary Barrum Ogle
Patricia Massen Oidtman
Elfriede Horninger Olney
Alice Rabius Opfer
Barbara Joseph Orenstein
Jean Bird Orr

Melinda Wagner Padgett
Martina Dittmer Pallette
Linda Rowland Palmer
Lynn Meyer Pannell
Yvonne Wommer Pardeu
Merrilyn Roller Parham
Bess Wells Paris
Sandra Shepard Parkhurst
Betty Veach Patrick
Bob Patterson
Sandra Johnson Patzman
Alice Hayward Pearson
Alma Kapplemann Peterson
Norma Jansen Phalen
Letha Haines Phillips
Lois Ehrlich Phillips
Barbara Hutchinson Pickering
Janice Bright Pinion
Anetta Michael Pitney
Peggy Moser Planck
Eileen Wade Plassmeyer
Anna Plott
Linda Stewart Pogue
Marilyn Yoffie Pollack
Geraldine Oesterly Popejoy
Linda Hedrick Porter
Barbara Elledge Potts
Arlene Suppes Powell
Johanna Jackson Powell
Joy Blades Powers
Betty Green Preis
Patricia King Preston
Susan Trainor Price
Patricia Jacobs Pulis
Henrietta Schlesinger Pung
Wilson Nathaniel Pyron, Jr.
Suzy Campbell Quick
Katy Adams Ragsdale
John Ralston
Sally Fuller Ramos
Joyce Honse Ramsey
Myla Walker Randolph
Mary Vollmer Rassieur
Catherine Ogden Rea
Dorris Smith Reed
Jane Sewald Regan
Benedette Gieselman Reh
Ruth Ann Ashmore Renick
Susan Keckeley Rentschler
Bee Allen Reynolds
Lisa Rhea
Betty Jo Atteberry Rice
Kathleen Willimann Rice
Coretta Thomas Richards
Richmond High School Nutrition
   Class, Paula Walden
Sue Standfer Riding
Elda Frerking Rist
Gloria Head Robbins
Carol Duncan Roberson
Margot McMillen Roberson

Mona Gibson Roberts
Charles F. B. Robinson
Judy Hollingsworth Robinson
Velma Robinson
Bonnie Fults Rodemich
Connie Canavan Roeder
Peggy Roller
Bethel Girvin Rone
Myra Faries Rone
Kris Flo Rose
Sharon Rich Rosenblum
Joyce Barnhart Rosenquist
Marian Levy Rosenthal
Jan Stewart Ross
Caroline Rowe
Rose Douglas Roweton
Susan Duncan Rozier
Elnora Montgomery Russell
Helen Butcher St. John
Bonnie Freisz Sanders
Janet Shelby Sanders
Almira Baldwin Sant
Charlotte Nabbefeld Sartori
Jeannie Harris Saunders
Virginia Wilson Savage
Shirley Lusher Schaefferkoetter
Janis Craig Schanbacher
Judy Harrison Schattgen
Kay Lamure Schilly
Elizabeth Schloman
Ellen Kirwan Schreiber
Anne Weigel Schultz
Nancy Katz Schwartz
Toni Sutor Schwartz
Norma Schweighoefer
Sally Fullerton Schwenk
Joyce Overholtzer Scott
Betsey Purnell Scruggs
Sheila Cox Searfoss
Karen Greenblatt Seigel
Katherine Flowers Seigfreid
Diane Dogotch Senkel
Phyllis Wagner Shapiro
Eleanor Michaelis Sharp
Sarah Hammack Sharp
Fern Runge Sherer
Arleen Motchan Shostak
Janice Boyer Siebert
Sheryl Greenblatt Silverman
Marcee Waldman Silverstein
Julie Lutz Simmons
Betty Green Sims
Patsy Merck Sims
Sue Stout Sims
Martha Magee Singleton
Kathryn Jones Skaggs
Margaret Skillman
Ethel Walls Smallwood
Connie Smith
Gail Heller Smith
Ina Rich Smith

Margaret Billings Smith
Martha Hendrickson Smith
Nancy Isenhowser Smith
Shirley Struely Smith
Tammy Stiles Smith
Jane Soendker
Constance Odom Soper
Connie Wieck Sorkin
Margie McCallister Souchek
Betty Dodds Soutern
Dorothy Menzel Sparks
Floreine Price Spilman
Barbara Nixon Sprong
Wilda Wise Stacey
Katherine Walton Staley
Vida Loberg Stanard
Carol Jean Stand
Mary Sue Patton Stansberry
Mary Crookshanks Staton
Ann Kelly Steele
Judith Brown Steiner
Cheryl Dunlop Steinkamp
Linda Boyce Steward
Byron Stewart, Jr.
Janet Lohoefener Stidman
Deborah Wimpee Stinnett
Edna Kallmeyer Stock
Ethel Rathert Stock
Ruth Stocksdale
Judy Peterson Stokes
Genevieve Miller Stonner
Rita Spence Stonner
Harriett Hard Story
Virginia Love Stout
Eleanor Rowland Strain
Carolyn La Barge Sudekum
Gail McMonigle Tangora
Jessie Stever Taylor
Joyce Thoeni Taylor
Jean Dingwerth Teel
Karen Jigewaelter Thaman
Kay Hiebert Thomas
Sonja Holland Thomas
Rita Ganahl Thuesen
Mary Carter Thurman
Florilla Frieze Tiona
Judith Smith Tisch
Catherine Thomson Todd
Joan Fulkerson Tompkins
Marianna Mayer Toombs
Johanna Schwarting Torrence
Edith Rinehart Trullinger
Agnes Simpson Turnbaugh
Betty Jane Rathbone Turner
Janet Lefevre Turner
James Turner
Lois Anne Turner
Merle Ferrier Turner
Phyllis Reeder Turner
Betsy Blattner Tutt
Catherine Carter Twitty

Carol Berger Van Dyke
Dorotha Moxley Vaughn
Robert Vaughan
Sharon Roderick Vaughn
Carol Jones Veron
Barbara Vineyard
Shirley Graham Vineyard
Janet Wilson Walker
Dana Dooley Walstad
Alice Dolinsky Walter
Rosemary Antwiler Walthall
Janet Neumeyer Ward
Lynn Teller Watkins
Jan Webber
Dorothy Bremer Weber
Melanie Thompson Webster
Susan Tiemann Webster
Barbara Logan Weems
Sharon Hestand Weinbrenner
Nancy Holstrom Werbach
Cathy Cordell Werner
Susan Snow Werries
Dottie Collins Wesberg
Sharon Douglas Westfall
Myrna Beck Wetzel
Susie Heard Wetzel
Ann Henslee White
Betty Bennett White
Clara Fricke White
Marjorie White
Irma Horman Whitlock
Evelyn Cox Whitworth
Georgiana Dickey Wiles
Betsy Kuntz Williams
Emily Gordon Williams
Phoebe Bibb Williams
Beth Boswell Willis
Betty Russell Willyard
Joan Murphy Wolken
Elizabeth Swarts Wood
Gail Shull Wood
Blanche Reeves Woodiel
Jan Stewart Woods
Laura Jane Joyce Workman
Grace Taylor Wormington
Kaye Hurley Worthington
Barbara Toombs Wright
Betty Wright
Dorothy Meyer Wright
Edith Darby Wright
Margie Carter Wynn
Raye Hillebrand Wyss
Cleta Ghere York
Connie Slavo Yorke
Claudia Finley Young
Genie O'Boyle Young
Jane Clinton Young
Lucille Marlin Young
Nancy Yuille
Alyce Schmidt Zerr
Reba Wade Zimmerman

BIBLIOGRAPHY

Books

Brownlee, Richard S. *Gray Ghosts of the Confederacy.* Louisiana State University Press, Baton Rouge, 1958.

Bryan, John Albury. *Missouri's Contribution to American Architecture.* St. Louis Architectural Club, St. Louis, 1928.

Constant, Alberta Wilson. *Paintbox on the Frontier: The Life and Times of George Caleb Bingham.* Thomas Y. Crowell, New York, 1974.

Croy, Homer. *Jesse James Was My Neighbor.* Duell, Sloan and Pearce, New York, 1949.

Giffen, Jerena East. *First Ladies of Missouri.* Von Hoffman Press, Inc., Jefferson City, 1970.

Larkin, Lew. *Missouri Heritage.* American Press, Inc., Columbia, 1968.

McReynolds, Edwin C. *Missouri: A History of the Cross-Roads State.* University of Oklahoma Press, Norman, 1962.

Morrow, Kate S. and Park, Eleanora G. *Women of the Mansion: Missouri, 1821-1936.* Midland Printing Company, Jefferson City, 1936.

Mumford, Lewis. *The Brown Decades: A Study of the Arts in America, 1865-1895.* Dover Publications, New York, 1971.

Pickard, John. *Report of the Capitol Decoration Commission: 1917-1928,* Hugh Stephens Press, Jefferson City, 1928.

Reed, Henry Hope and Tunnard, Christopher. *American Skyline.* New American Library, New York, 1956.

Rosenberg, John D., editor. *The Genius of John Ruskin.* George Braziller, New York, 1963.

Settle, William A. *Jesse James Was His Name.* University of Missouri Press, Columbia, 1966.

Miscellaneous

Abele, Mary Pat, "Missouri First Ladies . . . A Personal Perspective," Missouri Mansion Preservation, Inc., Jefferson City, 1980.

Hobbs, Myrene Houchin, "The Jefferson City Story," Cole County Historical Society, Jefferson City, 1956.

Murphy, Downey, Wofford and Richman/ Architects, "The Missouri Executive Mansion: A Long Range Development Study," Missouri Mansion Preservation, Inc., St. Louis, 1976.

Priddy, Bob, "Remembered in Jefferson City." *Missouri Life,* Vol. 11, No. 1 (March-April 1983), 37-39, Columbia.

Index—History

Recipes by Sections

Recipes by Alphabetical Listing